CYCLING *without* TRAFFIC: LONDON

Simon Forty

DIAL HOUSE

First published 2000

ISBN 0 7110 2705 6

© Simon Forty 2000

Published by Dial House

an imprint of Ian Allan Publishing Ltd, Terminal House, Shepperton, Surrey TW17 8AS.
Printed by Ian Allan Printing Ltd, Riverdene Business Park, Hersham, Surrey KT12 4RG.

Code: 0004/E

Picture cedits
All pictures by the author unless credited otherwise.

Front cover: London changes day to day and cycling around the city is the best way to watch the changes taking place: this is a view of a modern ley line — the Thames Barrier, Millennium Dome and Canary Wharf in conjunction.

Title page: Contemplating Epping Forest.

This picture: Which way to go?

Cycling is a superb way to get around, with the advantages outweighing any disadvantages — furthermore it improves health, fitness, co-ordination and awareness. It is energy-efficient: someone cycling uses one fifth of the energy of someone walking. It is often quicker than alternative forms of transport, especially in congested urban areas, for cyclists are less affected by heavy traffic flows — and journey times are thus more consistent and predictable than those made by car. Its impact on the environment is minimal, making cycling the most eco-friendly form of transport. By taking to the bicycle you can make a positive contribution to improvement of the environment through the consequent reduction of congestion and pollution from emissions and noise. Other great bonuses are cheapness and durability — a bicycle costs a fraction of the price of a car and with a little basic maintenance can last a lifetime. They are compact and versatile and used worldwide for work and pleasure. All-in-all, cycling is the most efficient form of personal transport on the planet!

However, there are disadvantages too, as anyone who has cycled home from a job in London on a wet, windy, winter evening will testify. It's a busy world out there, particularly in urban areas whose roads were not designed to be used by thousands of cars, so you need to be very careful. While the Cycling Without Traffic series was designed to supply the reader with routes that would allow vehicle-free cycling, any book covering the London area is bound to include some cycling along roads — and until local and national government really take cyclists into account, cycling on roads in London will be something to be undertaken cautiously.

To begin with, you must cycle legally. While the empty pavement is obviously safer than the congested road, you're not allowed to cycle on it unless it is signed as shared with pedestrians; the same is true of

Above: **Most London cycling involves traffic and all the problems that go with it.**
London Cycling Campaign/Tony Annis

empty footpaths and many other obviously cyclable public rights of way. While many people ignore 'No Cycling' signs and cyclists can be found mingling with pedestrians without causing any problems, they are cycling illegally and so can be penalised. Many of the locations and routes identified in this book have areas and sections where cycling is prohibited; indeed, many of the best off-road rides in London are out of bounds. The author does not suggest that the reader breaks the law, and where 'No Cycling' is indicated, even on perennially empty footpaths early on summer mornings, the cyclist should dismount and walk. It is through the illegal and irresponsible actions of a minority of cyclists that so much terrain has been made cycle-free. Do keep your eyes open even on familiar paths as the rules can change — often it seems without warning.

On the road, the same is true: you must cycle legally. The tempting shortcut — the wrong way up a one-way street — could not only lead to an accident and prosecution, but also could have a serious effect on insurance payouts. It's difficult enough to get fair treatment as a cyclist in British courtrooms without shooting yourself in the foot as well! In general, on the road the same laws apply to all road users — although increasingly there are more signs specifically directed at cyclists — and a thorough perusal of the Highway Code regulations is recommended. However, rules and regulations don't mean anything when an unprotected cyclist comes up against a badly driven car or lorry, and so cyclists need to be doubly careful of hazards when cycling on road. There's a simple, although unpalatable, dictum: if in doubt get off and walk your bike.

Motorists are certainly the major hazard: enclosed within a tough skin of powered metal they are prone to blind spots,

personality problems and impatience, as well as general inattention. Many of their actions can prove fatal to someone less armoured. It is a discouraging fact that over 30,000 people were killed or injured on British roads in 1998 and many of them were cyclists. You must, therefore, cultivate awareness, being both alert and assertive. Think ahead whilst cycling; anticipate the actions of other road users and try to make eye contact in order to make everyone clearly aware of your intentions and actions. Ride positively by keeping as much as possible to a straight line, looking and signalling in turn before any manoeuvre. Often, poor road surfaces cause cyclists to shift erratically: try to avoid this as it is a major cause of accidents. Motorists in right-hand drive cars spend more time looking at what's going on in front and to their right than looking at the kerb. Make sure you are easily visible at all times and take special care at night — wear something bright and reflective and cycle with lights. I emphasise this because cyclists wearing dark clothing and cycling without lights fitted are cycling illegally and are an accident waiting to

Below: **If you can get away from the roads: there are many cycleways which can make your journey to work considerably less stressful.**

happen. Ensure that you have lights if you're cycling after dark, that both front and rear lights are functioning, and that you have a red rear reflector. You may feel highly visible on a road lit by streetlights, but for a fast-driving motorist this isn't necessarily so.

That's enough about the obvious enemies; other disadvantages for urban cyclists are the same as those for anyone cycling — the vagaries of the British weather, lack of suitable amenities for cyclists in the work environment (protected parking, changing facilities, etc) and mechanical defects. We can't do much about the amenities other than lobbying; weather protection is also straightforward, if occasionally expensive; but mechanical defects are less obvious and sometimes more difficult to fix. The key rules are to treat your bicycle as you would a car: check it over quickly before you use it (particularly if use is infrequent), keep it clean and get it serviced regularly. One thing is essential: your bike must be the right size. It will be safer, easier and more comfortable if it is. Also crucial is the distance between saddle and pedal: it makes all the difference in the world to power generation, ensuring maximum power from minimum energy expenditure.

If you have just started cycling, or are restarting after some years' absence, don't overload yourself — take a bit of time to build up your stamina, your leg muscles and get used to sitting on a saddle. It is often the latter that curtails cycling trips rather than tiredness. Choose your terrain with care, perhaps starting with simple, predominantly flat, routes before riding rougher off-road tracks or up hills. As with all fitness training, one should start slow and small and escalate as your general level of stamina rises.

Leisure cycling is a mammoth growth area, complete with routes, cycle tracks and stadia, cycle centres and ancillary workshops and support organisations. Whether you want to develop by yourself or take part in group activities, there is a wide spectrum of choice that is increasing daily: it will only get better in this new millennium, as the problems of transport and pollution dictate a radical rethink on the way we get around. Even now momentous changes are taking place, as organisations such as the London Cycle Campaign and Sustrans radically increase the profile of cycle transport and the London boroughs construct the infrastructure of the London Cycle Network. The Government is involved, too, sanctioning this inevitable change, though it will require deeper rethinking in more areas — especially in official recognition, encouragement and finance, as well as increased provision for cyclists on the part of councils and railway/public transport companies. In reality, not a lot of these changes will come willingly. It is hard to understand why the railways do so little to encourage cyclists, a natural ally in the face of the large, powerful and rich motor transport lobby. A light in the darkness, however, is provided by the example of the 'Rolling Cycleway', the cycle-friendly Gospel Oak–Barking line.

Finally, the author and publisher have made every effort to ensure that the information quoted in this book is accurate and up to date but cannot accept any liability if the information is incorrect. Readers are advised to check details themselves before setting out on any of the routes as opening times, public transport links, etc, are liable to change.

Acknowledgements
Many people have contributed to this book and I'd like to thank them all, particularly my brother Jonathan and my wife Sandra who helped me write it, and routemeister Richard Wood with whom I cycled most of it. Thanks, too, to the cycle officers of all the boroughs that provided information, and those in other organisations like Sustrans and the LCC. I would like to thank Robert Smith for his excellent maps for each route.

Simon Forty
Kingston Upon Thames, February 2000

The Law

Off-road there are more than 120,000 miles of rights of way in the UK, but under the Countryside Act of 1968 cyclists are allowed on only 10% of them. These are bridleways, byways open to all traffic (BOATs) and roads used as public paths (RUPPs). Cycling where there is no right of way is illegal and so when using all the other 90% of such routes you can only walk the bike. Councils and Park Authorities, along with other public and private bodies, make public provision for access to their property and their rules and by-laws must be followed. In some cases, such as the British Waterways-owned canal paths, the amount of bike-access paths available has been assessed at 10%, for which a permit is required, which they will issue free. In the event of any conflict arising with a private or public landowner always remain absolutely calm and make a note of your location. The Rights of Way Department of the local authority will contain detailed local maps that can clear up any confusion.

The Country Code

■ Respect the countryside, the wildlife and local people who work in it.
■ Only ride where you are legally entitled to do so.
■ Always give way to horses and pedestrians.
■ Take special care on country roads.
■ Take all litter home with you.
■ Guard against all risk of fire.
■ Use and fasten all gates and stiles to cross fences, hedges and walls.
■ Keep dogs under close control.
■ Leave livestock, crops and machinery alone.
■ Help keep all water clean. Do not pollute watercourses.
■ Protect wildlife, plants and trees.
■ Make no unnecessary noise.

City Cyclists' Off-road Code

■ Always be prepared to slow down and stop.
■ Don't cycle on the pavement.
■ Always give way to pedestrians.
■ Carry a bell and use it — don't surprise people.
■ Where there is a dividing line between pedestrians and cyclists stay in your correct section.
■ Be especially cautious at blind spots such as at junctions, bends, entrances and near obstructions such as roadworks.
■ If visibility is poor use your lights and wear reflective clothing.
■ Be alert. Avoid the need for emergency braking on wet and slippery surfaces.
■ Insure against theft, liability and personal injury. The Police can postcode your bike as a security measure free of charge — ask at your local police station.

Accidents

Less than one in five accidents involving a bicycle are the fault of the cyclist. When you've been involved in an accident, stay very calm and admit no blame. Take down all the details and get in touch with a solicitor to claim compensation. They will usually be able to help on a no-win, no-fee basis. The London Cycling Campaign (LCC) will be able to provide contact names and numbers. Third-party insurance is offered by both the LCC and CTC (Cyclists Touring Club) as part of their membership. (See Appendices.)

London Cycling Campaign

With over 9,000 members, the London Cycling Campaign is the largest urban cycling lobby in the world. The LCC exists to promote cycling in Greater London for the benefit of individuals, local communities and the wider environment by raising awareness of cycling issues, campaigning to improve conditions for cyclists and providing services for its members. The LCC's local groups thus monitor their councils and boroughs, constantly tracking their performance and publicising their mistakes and indifference in order to achieve results. They are non-party political and their activities are non-violent, non-discriminatory and environmentally responsible. They network actively with a wide range of related organisations, working closely with other cycling, sustainable transport and environmental groups. Their specific aims to be achieved by the year 2000 are:

1. To ensure that cycling is a key part of a sustainable transport system that prioritises walking, cycling and public transport, and includes integrating cycling with public transport.
2. To ensure that a significant proportion of car journeys under five miles shift to cycling.
3. To ensure that the London Cycling Network is completed to a high standard and complemented by routes to local amenities.
4. To achieve the strict enforcement of relevant laws which protects cyclists' rights; effect changes to current and proposed legislation and identify new legislation which would further improve conditions for cyclists.
5. To ensure that the needs of cyclists are provided for in all stages of land use, transport planning and design.
6. To achieve a level of safety for cyclists throughout London which is sufficiently high to enable children to use cycles for school and recreational journeys.
7. To reduce the number of cycle thefts and increase the rate of recovery of stolen cycles.

LCC publishes a bi-monthly magazine — *London Cyclist* — and also *On Your Bike*, a definitive guide packed with accumulated cycling experience which helps riders to get the most out of cycling in London. Equally useful as a beginner's guide or a handy reference for the experienced cyclist, *On Your Bike* includes the Central London Cyclist's Route Map, covering Highbury to Streatham, and Hammersmith to the Isle of Dogs.

Membership of the LCC gives discounts in 50 bike shops, free legal advice, free third-party insurance, free *London Cyclist* magazine, optional personal accident and theft insurance, maintenance workshops, active campaigns and cyclists' route maps.

Details of its address and a borough-by-borough contact list are in the Appendices at the back of this book.

The LCC is an indispensable organisation and should be joined by all London cyclists! The bigger it is are, the more clout it has!

Below: **London Cyclist** — the magazine of the London Cycling Company.

www.lcc.org.uk/lcc

london cyclist

12.1999/1.2000 the magazine of the london cycling campaign £1.50 / free to members

BONDI

londoners who cycle *during* work

soho pedicabs

choosing the best cycling stocking stuffers

plus: future visions . . . professional panniers . . . awards for good cycling design

Sustrans

Sustrans is a civil engineering charity which designs and builds routes for cyclists, walkers and people with disabilities. Sustrans — Sustainable Transport — is an invaluable organisation at the front edge of a future transport culture which is ecologically sustainable for the dual purpose of health and the limitation of serious pollution from motorised traffic. In Continental Europe, where cycling is a more widespread and accepted form of transport, these facts have already been taken on board, with a correspondingly responsible and progressive attitude from governments and authorities. Research reveals the facts that road traffic has doubled within the last 20 years and that Britain now has the most densely trafficked roads in Europe, yet half of all car journeys are under two miles. Even a proportion of these carried out by cycle instead of car would have a significant effect, making the population fitter, more aware and communicative and the environment safer for all. Empowered with this wise motivation, Sustrans works on practical schemes to encourage people to walk and cycle more. With an eye cast nationwide through both country and city it is striving to realise a cycle network and link it all together in a practical way.

The National Cycle Network is Sustrans' baby — 3,500 miles of on-road and traffic-free routes to be in place by midsummer 2000, with 12,875km (8,000 miles) planned by the year 2005. The network consists of miles of traffic-free canal towpaths and disused railways, traffic-calmed and signposted quiet roads, and protected roads with special junctions and road crossings. It will also link local cycling networks and town centres all over the country and make many new routes. It is designed to be used for work, school, shopping and leisure, and to pass within two miles of 20 million people. It is a major Millennium Commission project and Sustrans' considerable and ever-growing public support has enabled it to receive a Millennium grant of £43 million to help realise the project. Hundreds of partner bodies, including local authorities, countryside and transport bodies, are also funding and implementing routes.

Sustrans has an updated web site that keeps its members informed, as well as newsletters and reports. It aims to quadruple the numbers of cyclists in the next few years,

Left: Sustrans is a national movement dedicated to the issue of developing sustainable transport — and in particular cycling.

develops relationships with Government departments to have a say in policy, helps co-ordinate cycle industry companies and seeks to find partners in route development. These include tourist agencies, railway boards, the Forestry Commission, the National Trust, English Heritage, British Waterways, the Cyclists Touring Club (CTC) and the British Cycling Foundation. Over 400 local authorities are already involved.

Other schemes include the Slower Speeds Initiative for motorised traffic and the Safe Routes to School project, emphasising the schoolchild's journey, which has also now been recognised and promoted by the Government.

Sustrans' reports and local offices divide the country into Scotland, the North East, the North West, Yorkshire, the Midlands, East England, London, the South East, Wales and South West England, and Northern Ireland, with its head office in Bristol (see Appendices). Sustrans also has an International section. Its routes are detailed by the Ordnance Survey, which now includes the National Cycle Network on its maps. Sustrans also publishes full specialist maps and guides, including Safe Routes to Schools, technical, accessory and information sheets, a financial report and a catalogue.

In these ways Sustrans is constantly trying to improve the quality of experience possible on the national route. 'Ride the Net', Sustrans' Millennium celebration and the inaugural ride on the National Cycle Network, is set for June 2000.

Sustrans will hustle, inspire, encourage and extol you to participate but that is as it should be, for only by taking the responsibility and making the effort will we change transport culture.

The core aim of the National Cycle Network is to connect urban centres and the countryside nationwide and to provide a safe, attractive high-quality network and a major new amenity for walkers and wheelchair users as well as cyclists. At least half of all routes will be made up of traffic-free sections such as disused

railways and watersides. The other half will use on-road sections such as minor roads and traffic-calmed stretches. All will be signed, mapped and suitable for an unaccompanied 12-year-old to cycle. Traffic-free sections will even be suitable for the very young.

This eco-friendly infrastructure will have many benefits and green tourism will generate rural income. Historic landmarks including canals, bridges, viaducts and old railways are being given a new lease of life by being linked into the route. There is even sculpture and milepost art!

Every cyclist and pedestrian should join Sustrans because it is an intelligent, positive, public-based institution that is actually fulfilling its purpose, with genuine benefit to all.

London Cycle Network
The London Cycle Network is a plan to develop over 2,414km (1,500 miles) of local cycle routes throughout London over the next five years. These routes will form a London-wide network which aims to make cycling attractive and safe to as many people as possible across the capital. It will provide direct access to all major centres of employment, education, leisure and all railway stations. All the London local authorities have a cycling officer and many produce local cycling maps and hold their own training and safety schemes (see Appendices).

As one of the biggest cycling schemes in the country, it is fully endorsed by government, local authorities and the business community. The network includes some of the National Cycle Network and regional routes being developed in and around London. It will consist of safe, segregated, signed cycle routes, where possible alongside or parallel to main roads. There will be special crossings at main road junctions, feeder lanes at many traffic lights and an advanced stop line to make cyclists more visible to other traffic. Some sections of the network will be along quieter minor roads where traffic flows are much slower. Other routes will be away

THIS IS THE LONDON CYCLE NETWORK

Above: An explanation of the London cycling network, complete with contact names and addresses for the different boroughs.

from roads completely, on paths across parks and on some footways alongside roads. Shared use with pedestrians will only be authorised where it is safe.

The whole network will be signed by blue and white signs to make it easy to follow through London's dense road network. Maps will be published to enable journey planning.

Cycle parking facilities will be increased at railway and tube stations, in shopping centres, and at schools, hospitals and leisure facilities. The specific cycle facilities to be introduced as part of the London Cycle Network will depend on local circumstances and priorities in individual boroughs.

As the network develops, and more routes are provided and signed, more people will be attracted back on to their bicycles. This is an ongoing process, and a steering group based in Kingston Upon Thames is co-ordinating efforts to realise the project and ensure that routes are coherent and continuous. This involves encouraging and interfacing with local councils and councillors, policy or decision makers, transport providers as well as education providers, employers and businesses.

By encouraging people to cycle rather than use their cars huge savings can be made, not least because healthier employees are more productive and take less time off work!

The London Cycle Network Project Manager is John Lee, employed by the Royal Borough of Kingston Upon Thames; he reports to the LCN Steering Group.

Canals and Towpaths

You need a permit to cycle along all British canalsides and towpaths. Permits covering all British Waterways except the Kennet & Avon are available free from:

British Waterways
The Toll House
Delamere Terrace
Little Venice
London W2 6MD

Phone: 020 7286 6101
Fax: 020 7286 7306

Enclose an A5 self-addressed envelope with a (currently) 39p stamp along with the full names and addresses of all persons for whom a permit is required.

Above: An introduction to London's canals including useful addresses and information.

Left: British Waterways leaflet explaining its aims and providing details of how and why to become a member.

The Boroughs

The London boroughs have varying degrees of enthusiasm for the city-wide cycle network, manifested in the routes they have developed and put in place. This is obviously affected by their location and environment, but also by their attitude and transport policies. Some (Hackney, Haringey, Kingston Upon Thames) have pioneered safer cycle provision within their jurisdiction and have joined the steering group that is co-ordinating the efforts to build the London network. Others shirk their responsibilities and continue to prioritise motorised traffic.

Above: On the Thames towpath at Hampton.

Left: Always dismount and walk around locks: usually barriers are made across the towpath to enforce this.

Above: Typical metal barrier across a canalside towpath; they are principally designed to stop motorcycles.

Most of the boroughs produce their own cycle maps as well as the London-wide London Cycle Network prototype now being introduced. Indeed, as a result of this, some are now phasing out their own, but the present LCN map is still a bit rudimentary and reflects the nebulous dream potential of the route, as well as being more of an overview. Local maps can be much more detailed. Most boroughs have a transport policy that aims to encourage walking and cycling, and reduce traffic congestion and pollution. Some are much hotter on achieving this than others and include in their local leaflet details of routes, cycle shops, addresses to report potholes and road damage, as well as promoting walking and cycling through the provision of facilities for providing training and education for cyclists, courses on cycle maintenance, basic riding skills and knowledge of the Highway Code (see Appendices for borough addresses and contact numbers).

Concerning the actual infrastructure, the boroughs have been putting in the following provisions towards the realisation of the network:

Advanced Stop Lines
Advanced stop lines are to help cyclists through traffic signals by allowing them to move ahead of other vehicles — thus they are more easily seen and less likely to be hit. These are clearly signed for both motorists and cyclists.

Bus Lanes
Cyclists are permitted to use all bus lanes unless there are specific local problems and signs. It is now accepted London-wide that this should be so.

Contra-flow and With-flow
Contra-flows allow cyclists to travel safely along one-way streets in the opposite direction to the general flow of traffic, often avoiding other busy streets and cutting down journey time. They are often segregated by wide hatching and kerbing, and signed both at beginning and end. With-flow cycle lanes are also signed and marked, providing an area for cyclists travelling in the same direction as the flow of traffic, usually in locations where other measures cannot be implemented.

Cycle Exemptions
Cycle exemptions have been made at junctions and road closures to give cyclists an advantage over other vehicles. Care should be taken when rejoining the main traffic flow.

Above Left: A cycle route leaflet from Harrow.

Above Middle: Enfield borough has produced a commendably comprehensive cycle map of its borough.

Above Right: The London Cycling Campaign group network is based at Kingston Upon Thames and the borough also produces a detailed cycling map of the area.

Cycle Crossings
Cycle crossings are often provided where a cycle route crosses a busy road. These can be controlled (signal-controlled toucans) or uncontrolled crossings — such as central islands allowing busy roads to be crossed in two stages. Elsewhere, cyclists could be directed on to conventional pedestrian crossings, where

Left: Cycle lanes have made a big difference to urban areas.

they should dismount. Special facilities have been provided at some roundabouts too.

Toucan crossings are provided so that when the green cycle appears you may safely cross the road. On all other crossings (zebra and pelican) you must dismount and wheel your bike across.

Cycle Gaps
Cycle gaps are where traffic has been restricted by bollards, gates and barriers, but where provision has been made for cyclists with the inclusion of gaps (usually on either side) for them to pass through.

Cycle Lanes
Cycle lanes are alongside vehicle lanes. Dashed lines show advisory cycle lanes. Where marked by a continuous white line, other vehicles are prohibited except in emergencies. Mandatory cycle lanes, exclusively for cyclists, are marked by a solid white line with a cycle logo. Advisory cycle lanes are marked by a dashed line and cycle logo.

Cycle Parking
Cycle parking has been upgraded and provided in town centres and shopping areas. Always be prudent and take precautions against theft by locking your cycle in a cycle rack or to some other street furniture.

Cycle Routes (Signed and Unsigned)
These signed and unsigned routes are designed to find safer and more pleasant ways around the boroughs — through parks and alongside rivers and canals, avoiding major road junctions and steep hills.

Cycle Tracks
Cycle tracks give cyclists their own section of road, free from other traffic and pedestrians. They often form bypass routes around potential hazards.

Shared-Use Paths
The conversion of footpaths through open spaces provides an attractive alternative to busy roads. National research has shown that there are very few reported injuries and accidents involving cyclists and pedestrians on designed shared-use facilities, so another way of protecting cyclists from traffic is provided by shared-use paths, where cyclists and pedestrians can mix safely. Where there is a white line to separate cyclists from pedestrians each may keep to their designated half. However, cyclists should not cycle on pavements or paths which have not been signed and converted to shared use.

Bikes on Trains
Many of the routes identified in this book assume that the reader is arriving by train, much the most sensible option in a crowded city and one that would be much easier if the railways were more considerate to cyclists. As a rule, the older trains (slam-door stock) heading west still have a van for bikes. The modern units don't and this can be very inconvenient for both cyclists and other passengers — particularly as a journey of any distance will mean carrying bikes over footbridges, up and down stairs and, once aboard, moving the bikes away from the doors each time a station is reached. Readers are advised to contact the appropriate Train Operating Company in advance to check whether there are any restrictions to bikes being carried on particular routes at certain times.

The London Cycle Network map details all overground stations, enabling the cyclist to plan longer trips by taking his/her bike on most local trains, though not during the 'rush hour'. For longer distances one should be able to book, with a fee of usually between £1–£3. On the Underground you can take a bike on surface lines and shallow tunnel lines, but again not during rush hour. Bikes are not allowed on any of the deepest tunnel sections of the system.

Bikes and Bike Hire
Whatever your purpose, aim or desire, there's a bike waiting for you somewhere, be it a BMX, a mountain or off-road bike, a racer, a tourer or a hybrid — a mixture of the previous types. Children's bikes exist in pretty much the same categories and have a few additions of their own. Nowadays, technology has improved performance with bikes getting constantly lighter and stronger with better gear and brake systems, quick release levers and seat

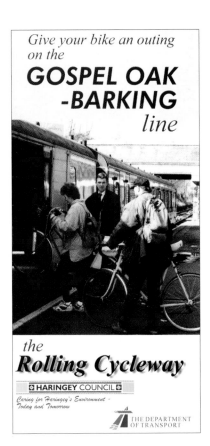

Give your bike an outing on the

GOSPEL OAK -BARKING
line

the
Rolling Cycleway

⊞ HARINGEY COUNCIL ⊞

Caring for Haringey's Environment - Today and Tomorrow

THE DEPARTMENT
OF TRANSPORT

Above: The Rolling Cycleway is endorsed by Haringey Council and this leaflet gives train times and other useful information.

You should glide along almost noiselessly, so tighten and adjust any parts that are loose or rubbing against any other moving parts. Lubricate your hubs, bottom bracket, chain, pedals, cranks and both sides of the gears. If there are still grinding sounds then the bearings have had it and should be replaced. Clean and replace all broken or worn parts and leave plenty of time if more serious shop repairs and servicing are required. Check for frame misalignment, or broken paint surfaces which could indicate a crack in the frame itself.

Above: Bicycles can be hired at many points around London. This particular one is at Richmond upon Thames.

design. The intrinsic design however remains the same and can't be beaten. Many popular areas for tourism now have bike-hire centres, most notably at large reservoirs and some Forestry Commission trails. They offer the opportunity to road test different kinds of bikes to find out what suits you best, to give non-cyclists a go, and to save you the trouble of transporting your own.

Bike Kit, Care and Maintenance
Your bike should be checked after each ride so that it is always freshly ready for blast-off next time. This does not require an expert. The four most important elements are the brakes, the wheels and tyres, the chain and the saddle.

Bags
There is a bewildering array of bags, panniers and carriers available for all types and sorts of cycling and cyclists. These range from the bike-mounted variety (front, back, side, top and sub-saddle) to man-mounted cycle sacks and belts.

Basic kit can be kept under the saddle or elsewhere on the bike, but from a security

Above: The author and cycling friends suitably dressed for a good days biking!

perspective you might prefer to carry everything on your own back, even though panniers, etc are detachable. It is important to ensure that the panniers are waterproof and secure on the frame.

Bell
Though there is a tendency for a bell to be seen as a historical artefact or fossil, it is in fact a very useful tool to warn others of your approach. Fit one and use it!

Bottles
A frame-mounted bottle is a useful extra for longer journeys and is invaluable for carrying water in hot weather.

Brakes
Ideally brakes should be 1cm–2cm away from the tyre rim; any further than this and they need adjustment. When squeezed they should then close evenly on the rim. Remember to check your brake cables as they receive a lot of wear and tear, as do the blocks themselves — replace where necessary, definitely before they become badly worn.

Chain
Check that your chain is not slack, that it is well oiled and rotates smoothly. Individual links can be replaced with a link replacer key.

Computers
Bicycle computers are small, inexpensive and lightweight, keeping you informed of your speed and mileage with performance data while on the move. They are simple to use and fit and are of use to the enthusiast as well as the more serious biker.

Gears
Check that the gears are lubricated, working correctly and are clean and free of any obstructions.

Kit
Most books will tell you to take spoke keys and chain tools with you wherever you go. Actually there's no point in buying any of these things if you aren't proficient with them or are poor at DIY (like me). I only ever carry a puncture repair outfit and a pump but occasionally an Allen key, spanner or pair of pliers can also come in handy. What's really good is a mobile phone so that you can ring someone to pick you up or tell you where the nearest bike shop is. Also handy is a cycling companion who is Bicycle Repair Man in disguise. Failing either of these things, buy a good bike maintenance book, learn it, practice what you learn and go out and buy those cone spanners and bottom bracket extractors.

Lights
Check that the lights are functioning properly before you leave. Carry a spare bulb and batteries.

Mudguards
There are two schools of thought about mudguards: on the one hand they get clogged with mud and are pretty uncool if you're out in Epping Forest on the tracks; on the other hand, if you want to stop off at a pub or restaurant, the staff (and some of the clientele) may well look askance at the long stripe of muddy water dripping down your back and off your backside. Make your own choice!

Saddle

It's really important to get your saddle right, particularly if you're going to spend any time in it. Make sure the saddle is correctly adjusted — you should be able to touch the ground with your toes and yet be high enough for your leg to be almost straight when pedalling. The wrong height for your saddle will make your effort much less efficient and cycling consequently much harder work.

Toeclips

Things that attach you to your bike (toeclips and cycling shoes) are, again, a matter of taste. They certainly ensure that you benefit from the best-directed physical effort (which, of course, is why professionals use them). However, if you're cycling in town and having to stop regularly at traffic lights, etc, then they are just a pain.

Tyres

In soft off-road conditions fit fat, knobbly tyres; for town and on-road narrower, smoother ones will do. Inflate to the correct pressure, which is detailed on each

Below: **Every cyclist has their own favourite pieces of kit as well as their beloved bicycle.**

tyre. A lower pressure is best for off-road and a higher one for tarmac. Check that the tyre treads are not worn or split.

Wheels

Ensure that your wheels are tight and true. Scan the bolts holding the wheel to the frame — they should be tight. Many modern bikes now have quick-release wheels and these should be checked carefully to see that they are properly tight. Correctly closed, the quick-release lever will curve towards the wheel. Check the spokes — they should be firm and true, if not they can be tweaked using an inexpensive spoke key. They can be replaced by removing the tyre, unscrewing the spoke nipple with a screwdriver, and pushing the spoke out of its hole in the hub. Reversing the procedure installs a new one. Check also for buckled rims.

Clothing and Footwear

Clothing should be tight yet loose enough to encompass your stretch, or else stretchable. If wearing tracksuit-type leggings or trousers, ensure that they are tight at the ankle to prevent interference to the chain. Not all people want to wear lycra, and looser clothing ranges are just as popular.

Warm Weather

For 20°C (68°F) and above, lightweight gear which wicks away sweat from the body is suitable. This would typically consist of:

- A peaked cotton cap.
- Towelling headband/wristbands.
- Sunglasses.
- Short-sleeved cycle jersey.
- Lycra or looser shorts. Padded cycling shorts are usually worn without underwear to counter chafing, and are also beefed up and cushioned to support your gluteus maximus. Without doubt they are the best invention since soft lavatory paper.
- Mitts with padded palms to absorb shock and sweat. There's a nerve that runs through the palm of your hand and pressure on it is uncomfortable. Wear padded gloves and find the right position to counter this.
- Ankle socks.
- Cycling shoes or flat-soled trainers.

Cold Weather

Below 20°C (68°F) one should adopt a layering procedure: the colder it is the more layers are needed. When you have warmed up you can always peel off a layer.

- The legs should be covered with lycra tights/tracksters, but if it is colder than 10°C thicker thermal leggings are needed.
- Top thermal layer and windproof jacket. Thermal protection is also required for the head and hands.
- Woollen thermal hat and scarf.
- Windproof cycling jacket, or the more expensive Goretex jackets that allow moisture to escape.
- Full-length thermal gloves and socks.
- Waterproof ankle-length boots/overshoes.

Right: **Dedicated cycle lanes are much the safest places for children to cycle.**

Wet Weather

One thing that experience teaches you is that if you cycle for any length of time in the rain you will get wet — if only from the sweat and condensation generated by all the hermetically sealed layers of clothing

Below: **Ensure that children wear protective headgear.** *London Cycling Campaign*

you're wearing. My rule is simple: if it's warm enough wear shorts, if it's cold and wet think about an afternoon spent fettling the bike! In emergency conditions, plasticise yourself using black bin liners and shopping bags which you cut and pull over your head, step into and tuck into shoes!

■ Goretex-based gear certainly lets most moisture out but not in, and waterproof suits made of breathable fabric are undoubtedly the best but they are expensive.

■ Trousers need to be loose enough to allow the legs to move freely.

■ Overshoes or a light waterproof boot.

Footwear

You can use almost any flat-soled footwear on a bike, though professional kit is available for a variety of functions. These are designed to fit into the pedal, do without laces and generally morph you to your bike.

Safety

■ Wear bright and reflective clothing.

■ Use yellow plastic spacer arms or flags if carrying a child on a rear seat.

■ Use reflective strips on panniers, etc.

■ Use lights.

■ Fit reflective pedals.

■ Beware looking too much like a UFO as this can be ultimately confusing!

Helmet and Headgear

For some strange reason, helmets are a subject of controversy. Quite why is beyond me. More than half of all major cycling injuries involve the head; helmets can definitely reduce impacts — so wear one. It's always best to get one with adjustable pads so that you can wear a headband in summer, or in cold weather, when up to 20% of body heat is lost through the head, wear a woolly hat or balaclava under your helmet.

Security

Cycle theft is a major problem, so it is strongly advised that you get insurance. Many bike clubs and organisations, including the LCC, CTC and Sustrans, offer insurance to their members.

■ Note the frame number of your bike and encode — Police bike-coding projects are free.

■ Buy the best lock you can afford. What's the point in spending lots of money on the bike of your dreams and then protecting it with a cable lock? The best protection is by a 'U' or 'D' lock, usually with a frame-mounted bracket. Only criminals with top kit will penetrate this.

■ When leaving your bike, lock it to something immovable such as street furniture — railings, lamp posts, etc. Lock two bikes together instead of separately and use a chain to secure the wheels to the frame. Always remember to undo all quick-release parts and lock them to the frame or take them with you.

Children

Nowadays an ever-expanding industry represents and caters for children's needs. Under six years old they cannot travel too far on their own, but there exist many child seats or trailers to carry them in comfort and safety.

Refreshments

Beware the 'knock'! Your muscles are your engine, so keep them fuelled. Whether on longer trips or out only for the day, ensure you have some food with you. Dehydration is another danger to look out for — always travel with some liquid refreshment. Most bottles attach directly to the frame of the bike, within easy reach.

Final Check Prior to Blast-off:
Basic maintenance and repair kit.
Spare inner tubes.
Waterproofs.
Water bottle.
Sun cream.
Sunglasses.
Insect repellent.
Small medical kit.
Food and liquid.
Lock.
Money.
Cloth/wipes.
Lights and reflective gear.
Map/route book.
Mobile phone (if you've got one. If not take a phone card).

Transporting Your Bike

Modern car racks are excellent and transport bikes conveniently and easily. Just ensure that your back numberplate and lights are visible or you'll get pulled over. If necessary, get another plate made and fasten it to the bikes when in transit. Always think about protecting car surfaces from spiky or moving parts; always attach the bike to the car with bungees or rope; always remove anything not bolted on to the bike.

The advantages of a roof-mounted cycle rack are that the bike is well out of the way, the boot is still accessible, indicators and the back number-plates are unobscured, and, if transporting more than one bike, they are not resting against each other but held apart by the rack's design. The disadvantages are that you will use more fuel, the car will handle differently in crosswinds, you have to be quite tall in order to accomplish roof-mounting easily, and, if you forget, you can easily wipe the bikes out in low car parks!

Repairing a Puncture

To prevent punctures keep your tyres inflated to the recommended pressure, inspect them regularly for wear and tear and avoid sharp objects on the road such as broken glass. However, as well as exercising vigilance, always travel with a pump and a puncture repair outfit, which should contain patches, rubber cement, chalk, chalk grater (usually a prepared part of the repair kit box), wax crayon and sandpaper. A spanner to undo the nuts holding the wheel to the frame is essential, as are metal or plastic tyre levers. In fact, it is often better to carry a spare inner tube or two, so that one's journey is not too delayed. One can then install a fresh tube instantly and repair the original at a later, more convenient date. Some wet wipes or a rag to clean oily and dirty hands are also recommended.

If you do have to repair a puncture, this is the best procedure:

1.   First unhitch the brake cable, then remove the wheel using a spanner to undo the nuts holding it on to the hub if it is not fitted with quick-release levers.

2.   Check the tyre immediately to see if there is any obvious outward sign of the cause of the puncture. Off-road this will often be thorns or nails. Finding the location allows you to mark the spot before removing the tyre — very useful if there's no water around.

3.   Remove the tyre from the rim, using tyre levers if the fit is tight. Insert two levers under the rim a few inches apart and push on them together to free the tyre from the rim, taking care not to pinch the inner

Below: Smooth gear changing makes life much easier. *London Cycling Campaign/Jez Coulson/ Insight*

Above: **Both Bushy Park and Richmond Park are ideal for cycling, but stay legal.**

8. While you are waiting for the glue to set, check the inside of the tyre to ensure that the cause of the puncture has been removed. There's nothing more irritating than getting another flat because you missed the thorn that caused the problem in the first place. Additionally, it is not unusual to find more than one sharp object and if you do, you can mend the other hole without having to go through the whole process again in a few minutes!

9. When the five minutes are up, select the patch you are going to use, remove the foil and push the patch firmly into place over the puncture. Peel off the backing paper and press down firmly. Next, using the chalk in your kit, dust the area with some grated chalk. This stops the glue from adhering to the inside of the tyre.

10. Replace the tube inside the tyre by reversing the earlier process of removal. Ensure that the tube is not twisted and that it is completely inside the tyre — particularly near the valve. It is often helpful to inflate the inner tube slightly at this stage to ensure that it is fully inside the tyre and doesn't get nipped as you put the tyre back on to the rim.

11. Next, using only hand pressure, ease the tyre back on to the rim. The final section of it will be the hardest — use the heel of the palms and your thumbs to roll it back inside the rim.

12. Reinflate the tyre, replace the valve locking ring and the dust cap, then remount the wheel, ensuring that it is set centrally and the nuts holding it on to the hub are screwed up tightly. This can be checked by spinning the wheel while watching to see if it rubs against the frame. Reattach the brakes. Blast-off.

tube. Then work the levers around the rim until the tyre is completely free. In fact, with practice this can be done easily by hand.

4. Remove the dust cap and any locking ring from the valve, then push the valve through its hole in the rim and gently pull the inner tube out.

5. Partially inflate the tyre, checking first for a faulty valve, then pass the inner tube close to your ear or cheek to check for escaping air. You can almost always hear or feel it, but occasionally you might need to immerse the tyre in water to look for escaping bubbles of air. When you have located the puncture, mark it with a cross, using the wax crayon in the repair kit.

6. Deflate the tyre again by pushing in the valve. Hold it so that the section with the puncture is tight over your knuckles to deflate it fully. Using the sandpaper provided in the kit, lightly roughen the area around the puncture — this is to key it so that the two rubber surfaces will bond.

7. Spread the glue thinly over the puncture, covering an area slightly larger than the patch you have chosen to use, then leave it to dry for at least five minutes. This is the stage where many people go wrong, for they try to stick the patch down too soon. The glue is not an adhesive but is in fact melting the rubber in order to absorb the patch more fully.

Introduction

Although this book is primarily concerned with off-road cycling in London on pre-planned routes, there's no getting away from roads and traffic. I've found that Sunday morning cycling is the best answer, as is a mixture of quiet roads, off-road routes and pushing the bike when the traffic gets unacceptably busy. Interesting, gentle, discreet routes can be worked out with a little practice and experimentation by combining quiet backroads with off-road tracks and council cycleways. Look carefully at your maps (the Ordnance Survey Explorer and Landranger are recommended), publications such as *On Your Bike*, and go out and use trial and error! You'll have fun doing it, discover some great pubs and find much easy, hazard-free cycling that opens up the hidden back streets of London — criss-crossed with ancient transport infrastructures. A deceptive amount of London is navigable off-road, using the older transport systems of canal, railway and river. The Thames route is a separate entity on its own, but other rivers, streams, canals and waterways disgorge into Father Thames as well, and their sidepaths reveal the world of the water-roads. Though mixed-use does not allow them to be high-speed conduits, river paths are remarkably calm and tranquil, with a profile of nature panoramically displayed, truly *rus in urbe*! It is with these paths that we start our routes section.

Note on the route maps: Easily recognisable points along the route are numbered in the route instructions. These are also shown on the route maps.

Above: The River Police patrol the Thames, but it is rare for cyclists to come into contact with them.

The Thames

The Thames Cycle Route

A part of the National Cycle Network of specific concern to London is the Thames Cycle Route. Over three million people live within two miles of this route which penetrates through the very heart of London. Over 200 schools lie within a mile of it and there will be a high proportion of traffic–free sections, so thousands of schoolchildren will be able to cycle to school. The 71km (44-mile) route will forge a green link between the capital's premier traditional, tourist and Millennium sites and will be of immeasurable benefit to both commuters and tourists. Running from Hampton Court in the west to Thamesmead Town in the east, the route will present visitors with a unique succession of national sites and monuments including the Houses of Parliament, Tower Bridge, the Globe Theatre and the *Cutty Sark*. It will also link London's 'Millennium sites' at Bankside Power Station, the London Eye near the former County Hall, and the new South Bank Centre. The route will also link the Thames to rural Hertfordshire through the east and the north of London via the Lea Valley Pathway. To the south it will join to the Waterlink Way, taking cyclists to Gatwick Airport and beyond. Sections of this route are already in existence.

Work on the Thames Cycle Route is progressing well, with construction in the Richmond and Woolwich areas taking place during 1998–9. However, it is not possible to recommend a complete through-route yet, though it is possible to cycle from Putney Bridge to Hampton Court on the existing riverside path, and then on towards Weybridge in Surrey. Other open sections include routes in Richmond Park and around Thamesmead Town.

Sustrans is working in the capital with the London boroughs, the Environment Agency, British Waterways, Thames Water, English Heritage, the Royal Parks, the Cross Rivers Partnerships, the London Cycling Campaign, development agencies and many others. The National Cycle Network routes will also form a strategic part of the 1,500-mile London Cycle Network.

Above: **The magnificent view of the Thames from the top of Richmond Hill.**

Thames Police

The Thames has had its own official police force for over 150 years. There are more than 30 duty boats patrolling the Thames around the clock, plus three larger launches for the superintendents; most of these are based at Wapping. Known as Thames Division they have jurisdiction over 87km (54 miles) of river from Staines in Middlesex right down to Dartford Creek on the south bank and Havering on the north bank. The only floating police station in London is beside Waterloo Bridge on the north bank and known as Waterloo Pier.

The police enforce speed limits on the water (a blue light and siren are used to 'pull' offenders) as well as many other duties including drifting ships, collision incidents, fire on board ship, lost cargoes, dead bodies and flood warnings.

In times gone by the river was thronged with thieves, smugglers and scoundrels always on the lookout for a quick profit — especially around the busy dockyards and inadequate warehouses. Thus the Marine Police Force was founded in 1798 and was the first fully organised police force in the country. At the time, gangs of thugs stole as much as half of all the cargo entering London and as many as a third of the port workers themselves were involved in the thieving. The new force recruited tough seamen and boatmen to make a force of 200 armed men paid for by the government. They set to breaking up the gangs with vigour — often resulting in long-running bloody battles. They improved the situation but wholesale thieving was only stifled when the enclosed docks were built, each of which organised its own police force. In 1909 all the forces were gathered together under the Port of London Authority when they co-operated with the Metropolitan Police's Thames Division to become, in time, one force.

Above: Swans gather in large numbers on the Thames at Hampton — just down from Sunbury where the Swan Upping ceremony starts at the end of July.

Swans

Swans are protected in England and regarded as royal birds. According to legend, swans arrived here as a gift to Richard I from Queen Beatrice of Cyprus. Since then they have bred happily and thrived, protected as they are by severe laws. From 1496 it was decreed that every swan on every river in the kingdom be counted annually and a record made of the number. Henry VIII ordered the owners of swans to mark their cygnets with nicks on their beaks and any not marked would belong to the Crown. For many years only royalty and nobles were allowed to own swans, then City livery companies were granted the privilege, as was Eton College. Most of the swans on the Thames belong to the monarch or to the Dyers' and Vintners' companies. The monarch's swans since the Middle Ages have been looked after by the Keeper of the Swans. He presides over the ceremony of Swan Upping which has taken place since Elizabethan times at the end of July/beginning of August; the ceremony now takes place on the

last Monday in July, when, with the assistance of swanherds from the Dyers' and Vintners', he rounds up the new cygnets and marks their beaks with nicks — one for the Dyers', two for the Vintners' and none for the monarch.

The Swan Uppers dress for the occasion, the Queen's Swan Keeper in scarlet and gold, Vintners' in green and the Dyers' in blue. They then proceed up river over a period of a couple of days in a small flotilla of boats with banners flying, to 'up' the swans. The ceremony starts at Sunbury and ends at Pangbourne with a traditional banquet whose main dish is swan. Until 1980 the journey started at Temple Stairs, Southwark.

Right: No nocks on a swan's beak means that it belongs to the monarch.

HAMPTON COURT TO KINGSTON

(optional return through Bushy Park)

This is a gentle riverside cycle ride suitable for children. It can be busy — especially in the summer when the Hampton Court Flower Show takes place — with pedestrians, runners, dogs and other cyclists. It allows unparalleled views of the great royal palace of Hampton Court, particularly of the wonderful Wren façade and the Tijou Screen (see below).

PLACES OF INTEREST

Hampton Court Palace

Set in 24 acres (60 acres) of gardens, the original building was started in 1514 by Cardinal Wolsey, Chancellor to King Henry VIII. When the latter took possession of the buildings in 1526, he frequently installed the royal court there as it was an easy river trip from the polluted air of London. All of his six queens except the first, Catherine of Aragon, lived at the palace, which was used by succeeding royal families until the end of George II's reign; even Oliver Cromwell lived here while Lord Protector.

The great Tudor palace was enormously extended over a period of 11 years by the architect Christopher Wren who built a series of state apartments for William III. The Wren façade is best seen from the riverside, as are the magnificent 12 wrought iron panels known as Jean Tijou's Screen. They have recently been partially restored to their original glory. On the palace side of the screen is a modern recreation of the Privy Garden, of a type that would have been there in the past.

Much of the palace and most of the grounds (including the maze) are open to the public. To explore them and do them justice takes a good day: it is well worth the effort as Hampton Court remains the quintessential English royal palace. In 1997 an ambitious scheme to remodel the Palace Privy Garden was started.

Visitors winced as the area in front of the William and Mary façade, bordered by the Tijou screens, was ripped up and replanted. Today it is maturing nicely, and worth visiting.

Kingston Upon Thames

The oldest of the three Royal Boroughs of England, Kingston grew up around the ford that made it a strategic position on the Thames as well as a natural centre for trade and business. It was originally known as Moreford (the Great Ford), changing to Kingston in Saxon times. The ancient King's Stone outside the Guildhall marks the spot where various Saxon kings were crowned, including Edward the Elder and Ethelred the Unready. Kingston's oldest surviving charter dates back to the reign of King John in 1200. It was an important centre for the river industries of fishing and boat building and also the bulk industries of malting, milling and tanning that required river transport.

Having been an important market town since its beginning, in 1628 Kingston was granted an exclusive market charter by Charles I that protected it from competition. Aside from the Tudor façades in the market square, little now remains of the old town. Kingston Bridge was the first on the Thames above London Bridge until 1750; the present stone version was built in 1827.

Kingston was created a Royal Borough in 1927 and the county assizes transferred from Guildford in 1930, the same year the county council offices were opened and the town became the county town of Surrey. It is still a very busy shopping and business centre, and especially popular on its riverside in the summer.

Bushy Deer Park

Lying opposite Hampton Court is Bushy Deer Park, containing in its 445ha (1,100 acres) deer and many horse chestnut trees. The land was owned by the Knights Hospitallers of St John until 1514 when bought by Cardinal Wolsey, who enclosed it with high brick walls and stocked it with deer, pheasants and partridges. Henry VIII acquired Bushy Park at the same time as Hampton Court, regularly hunting and practising his archery there. At his death in 1547 the fences and walls were removed and the public given access.

The park was formalised by Christopher Wren who envisaged it as a grand chestnut avenue approach to Hampton Court Palace for William III. Originally sited in the Palace Privy Garden, the bronze statue in the centre of the round pond is the Diana Fountain, sculpted by Francesco Fanelli. In 1714 Wren had it removed, repaired, regilded and resited in Bushy Park.

Starting Points: Hampton Court railway station (1A) or car park in Bushy Park (1B).

Parking: In Bushy Park, Hampton Court Palace itself, or off the A308 in the direction of Sunbury and the M3.

Public Transport: South West trains run half-hourly (hourly on Sundays) to Hampton Court station — a 35min journey from Waterloo; the stops include Clapham Junction.

Links to Other Paths: Extend eastwards at Kingston on to Route 2. If you cross Hampton Court Bridge you can extend the path westwards along the Thames as far as you want! The path runs easily to Walton and Weybridge and further.

Distance: c4.5km (2¾ miles) Hampton Court Bridge to Kingston Bridge; round trip from station and back through Bushy Park c10km (6¼ miles).

Map: Explorer 161.

Above: The Thames-side frontage of the magnificent Jean Tijou wrought-iron screen.

Below: The Hanoverian frontage of Hampton Court Palace viewed from the Long Water.

Surfaces and Gradients: Flat as the proverbial pancake. All paths are either stone or metalled and only present any problems after heavy rain (deep puddles!).

Roads and Crossings: If you come from the station and don't enter Bushy Park, there are no roads to cross. The A308 (a busy road at all times) must be negotiated at Kingston and Hampton Court but in both places there are zebra crossings.

Refreshments: There are plenty of places in Kingston and around Hampton Court. Look out for the King's Head PH at the Lion Gate into Hampton Court (opposite the entrance into Bushy Park) and the White Hart PH at Kingston Bridge.

Route Instructions: 1A. From Hampton Court railway station cross the bridge and turn right (2) on to the metalled road alongside the palace.

or

1B. Exit Bushy Park at the A308 exit. Cross the road by the zebra crossing on your left and turn right following the palace wall. Go past the lavatories (excellent, and accessible from the road) and the entrance to the palace, turning left at the foot of bridge (2).

3. Follow the riverside path to Kingston.

4. Either retrace your path or turn left at the foot of Kingston Bridge and cross the A308 by zebra crossing. Turn right on to the B358 (Church Grove) for about 100yd. If you're in a hurry, return to Hampton Court along the A308 (there's a cycle lane).

5. Go through the metal gate into the tree-lined path leading to Bushy Park (entered by a second gate some 100yd further on).

6. Follow the path to the A308 exit and follow the instructions above. There's an excellent children's play area (sandpit, swings, etc) just before the A308 exit.

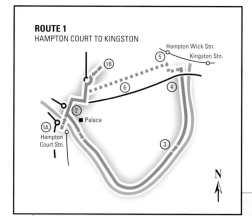

ROUTE 1
HAMPTON COURT TO KINGSTON

Hampton Wick Stn.
Kingston Stn.
Palace
Hampton Court Stn.
N

Below: The Privy Garden was restored with historic authenticity in the 1990s and has now grown up to be one of the finest formal gardens in England.

KINGSTON TO RICHMOND

(optional return via Twickenham)

Another gentle riverside cycle, this route can become quite exciting at high tide when the path between Richmond and Ham House can be thigh-deep in water! Very busy on summer weekends, it passes Teddington Lock (the first on the Thames), the exquisite Ham House and Quinlan Terry's splendid Richmond riverside development. If you are unlikely to return to the area, it is certainly worth detouring from this route to the top of Richmond Hill to look down over the great curve of the river towards Kingston (see Route 1).

PLACES OF INTEREST

Teddington Lock

The highest tidal point on the Thames and the last customs post on the river, there are three locks here: the Long Lock is for bigger barges and tugs. A short distance away lies the weir which prevents the tidal salt water mixing with the fresh river water — London Bridge is 32km (20 miles) away and high water is 1.5 hours later.

Ham House

Surviving unaltered in its beautiful riverside setting since the 17th century, Ham House was built in 1610 by Sir Thomas Vavasour, Knight Marshal to James I. It was then acquired in 1637 by William Murray, the first Earl of Dysart and remained in the family for the next 300 years. Its main period of expansion took place under the first earl's only child Elisabeth, who along with her second husband, the Duke of Lauderdale (the 'L' of Charles II's famous 'cabal' of advisors — Clifford, Ashley Cooper, Buckingham and Arlington were the others), completely redecorated at tremendous expense in the 1670s. Its interior decoration

remains one of the finest surviving examples of the Restoration period.

Petersham

At the foot of Richmond Hill lies the riverside village of Petersham, mentioned in the Domesday Book. In the 17th and 18th centuries it was a favourite resort of the nobility who built grand residences such as Petersham House, Montrose House and Elm Lodge, where Dickens later stayed while writing *Nicholas Nickleby*. Petersham Lodge was burnt down in the 1720s and redesigned and built as one of the first Palladian houses in England. The parish Church of St Peter has a 13th century chancel and a tower built in 1505, though the rest is of Georgian origin. Captain George Vancouver, who gave his name to the island off the Pacific coast of Canada which he discovered on his journeys with Captain Cook, lies buried here.

York House Gardens, Twickenham

Behind a high brick wall and parallel to the Thames lies an extraordinary fountain. Standing in a pool full of rocks and rushes, made of white marble and considerably more than life-size, is a statue of a naked girl with long flowing hair, surrounded by her equally bare sisters, some of them partially in the water. This was built by Sir Ratan Tate, the last private resident of nearby York House and an Indian merchant prince.

Above: **Footbridge over to Teddington from the Ham side of the river. There are two pubs on the Teddington side right by the pathway!**

Right: **Cycle way from Kingston town centre.**

Pope's Grotto

In 1719 renowned poet Alexander Pope moved to the Twickenham riverside where he leased a house that architect James Gibbs remodelled into a small Palladian villa. His main interest, however, was his garden, which was reputed to be one of the finest in England. There, lined with shells, semi-precious stones and mirrors, he built a grotto which in 1736 he opened to the amazed scrutiny of the public. Sophia, Baroness Howe, bought the house and grounds in 1807 but became so fed up with visitors coming to look that she had the house pulled down, the gardens destroyed and the grotto ransacked. Pope's exquisite underground grotto still exists, albeit a shadow of its former glory; it has been partially restored and is occasionally open to the public.

Marble Hill

Henrietta Howard (later Countess of Suffolk), the discreet mistress of George II, built Marble Hill in 1724 with money (£11,500 plus furniture and jewellery) he gave her and the help of Lord Herbert — an enthusiastic amateur architect who created an elegant Palladian villa — and local resident Alexander Pope who gave advice on the garden and park. It is said that Pope, while watching Henrietta open a parcel from Spain one day, saw some twigs fall from the package. He took them home, planted them and one grew the first weeping willow in England. Marble Hill declined into decay in the 19th century and was on the verge of being demolished. In 1901 it was saved and restored by London County Council, redecorating the rooms as originally conceived, and recreating as closely as possible the furniture, wallpaper and decorations.

Orleans House

Orleans House was built in 1710 for James Johnson, Secretary of State for Scotland under William III. All that remains of this original structure is the Octagon, designed by James Gibbs, standing in a woodland garden. The house acquired its present name after it became home to Louis-Philippe, the exiled Duke of Orleans, later King of France 1830–48. The house was pulled down in 1927 with the exception of the Octagon, which was rescued by the Hon Mrs Ionides who left it and her art collection to the borough.

Eel Pie Island

A narrow bridge is the only way on to this two-acre mid-Thames island, once famous for the eponymous rhythm and blues club where bands such as the Rolling Stones and the Yardbirds cut their teeth. The island still has a feeling of the 1960s and 1970s, with its small and often rather ramshackle bungalows and chalets.

Richmond Bridge

Richmond Bridge is London's only surviving pre-Victorian close-arched bridge; in fact, it is the oldest surviving bridge in Greater London — all the earlier central bridges having been rebuilt. It was built by James Paine and Kenton Couse in 1774–7 whose elliptical arched design was based on a Palladian bridge in Vicenza. It was widened and the gradient reduced in 1937, and at the same time an obelisk and toll houses on the Richmond side were removed.

Starting Points: Kingston railway station (1A) or Kingston's riverside car parks (1B).

Parking: Bentall's Centre or John Lewis multi-storey car parks; some riverside parking in front of Canbury Gardens. Note: Kingston is a very busy shopping centre, particularly at the weekends, and car parking space is at a premium.

Above: Richmond Bridge was based on a bridge in Vicenza and originally had a considerably higher gradient as well as an obelisk and toll houses.

Public Transport: South West trains run four times an hour (twice an hour on Sundays) to Kingston from Waterloo either on the Shepperton branch or the loop back to Waterloo via Twickenham and Richmond.

Links to Other Paths: This route joins Routes 1 and 3 (the Thames Paths) directly, and Route 16 (Richmond Park) by means of a slight detour.

Distance: c7km (4 miles) from Kingston railway bridge to Richmond Bridge. Returning via Twickenham and Teddington gives a c15km (9 miles) round trip.

Map: Explorer 161.

Surfaces and Gradients: No gradients unless a short detour is made to the top of Richmond Hill. Surfaces are excellent although some tide-borne flotsam can be difficult on the path at Petersham.

Roads and Crossings: Lower Ham Road after Canbury Gardens in Kingston (traffic-calmed using sleeping policemen; a very gentle road); Richmond Road on the Middlesex side after Richmond Bridge; some road use needed if optional return route via Twickenham and Teddington is taken.

Refreshments: Plenty of places in Kingston, Richmond, Twickenham and Teddington — look out for the Boaters at Kingston, the White Cross Hotel at Richmond, the Swan at Twickenham, the Pope's Grotto on the A310 out of Twickenham and the Anglers sited conveniently next to the footbridge above Teddington Lock.

Route Instructions: 1A. Turn right out of Kingston station and follow the pavement over the one-way system, going right under the railway bridge by the access road (Steadfast Road) to the multi-storey car parks, to the barrier on Skerne Road. Turn into Down Hall Road. At the bottom of the road turn right into Canbury Gardens (2).
or
1B. From the car parks push the bike along the pavement of Thameside to Canbury Gardens (2).

3. Follow the cycle path, turning left when it joins Lower Ham Road.

4. Join the Thames Path when Lower Ham Road leaves the riverside.

5. Follow the path to Richmond Bridge.

6. At the bridge either retrace your steps, return via rail from Richmond station (6A) or climb the steps to the roadway and cross the bridge (6B).

or

6A. The quickest way to Richmond station means going through Richmond itself (join George Street by turning right on to Water Lane in front of the White Cross Hotel; the station is on the right about half a mile away. A less crowded way is to go past the White Cross joining Friars Lane which exits on to Richmond Green. Follow the Green round, turning left to go past Richmond Theatre; there's an alleyway to the station alongside the railway bridge.

or

6B. Go up the steps to Richmond Bridge and cross to rejoin the riverside path on the other bank.

7. Follow the path past Marble Hill Park to Hammerton's Ferry (usually open in the summer — but don't count on it!) and cross back to the Surrey side, or continue on towards Twickenham.

8. Join the road (Riverside) and follow past Orleans Park, under the footbridge to York House and the entrance to York Gardens (at left), on to the Embankment.

9. Follow the road on to Cross Deep, the main road (A310) to Kingston.

10. Follow the A310 taking the left fork at the mini-roundabout just past Pope's Grotto, using the cycleway to Teddington.

11. Turn left on to Ferry Road and cross the footbridge above Teddington Lock.

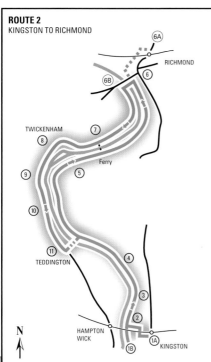

ROUTE 2
KINGSTON TO RICHMOND

6A
RICHMOND
6B
6
TWICKENHAM
8
7
Ferry
9
5
10
11
TEDDINGTON
4
3
2
N
HAMPTON WICK
1B
1A
KINGSTON

Below: York House was built by Sir Ratan Tate and is now used as local council offices.

33

RICHMOND TO KEW

(optional return via Syon House)

This is another gentle riverside cycle ride that joins the pretty town of Richmond and the world-famous botanical gardens at Kew. To make the return journey more interesting, take the Middlesex bank of the Thames through Syon Park (stopping off, perhaps, at Butterfly World or the house itself) before rejoining the river at Richmond Lock.

PLACES OF INTEREST

Kew Gardens

One of the greatest botanical gardens in the world, Kew Gardens occupies 121ha (300 acres). Within its walls are some of the most magnificent glasshouses anywhere containing collections of plants from around the globe, and a scattering of classic temples, ruins and buildings — including a pagoda begun in 1761. The Great Palm House, built in 1848, and the magnificent Temperate House (built 1860–98), were both designed by Decimus Burton. Each building has been thoroughly restored to its

Above: The magnificent glass Palm House designed by Decimus Burton is one of the prime attractions of Kew Gardens.

former glory in recent years. Kew is primarily a research institution where plants are studied for their properties and investigated for possible agricultural and medical use. It is also a scientific institution for the accurate identification of plants and a centre for the distribution of economic and decorative plant material. It is a leading institution in the worldwide fight to prevent the extinction of plant species.

Frederick, Prince of Wales (son of George II and father of George III) and his wife Augusta turned the grounds of their palace at Kew into a pleasure garden in the 1730s. After Frederick died, his widow Augusta, Dowager Princess of Wales, started to assemble a collection of foreign plants and trees in the then 3.6ha (9-acre) grounds. Her son George III loved Kew and took his court there and used the palace as his country residence. Sir Joseph Banks became Kew's unofficial director and under him the gardens gained botanic prominence, so much so that in 1841 a Royal Commission directed that it be handed over to the nation.

Richmond Tidal Barrage

The River Thames below Teddington is controlled by the Port of London Authority, and Richmond is the only lock on the river controlled by it. The lock is half tidal and used for tide control. The moveable weir and footbridge were built in 1894. For two hours on either side of high water the weirs are up and the river is fully tidal up to Teddington. Red discs (or lights) are visible under each arch when the weir is down. During the high spring and autumn tides the towpath and water meadows around Richmond frequently flood.

Syon House

Built as a nunnery for the Bridgetine Order in 1415 by Henry V and named after the holy hill of Sion in Palestine. The buildings were claimed by Henry VIII at the time of the Reformation (1534), although the nuns briefly returned when Queen Mary restored the old religion (Catholicism). Syon House was a valuable asset and passed from hand to hand with the changing powers. The doomed Lady Jane Grey was offered the crown of England here (she was queen for nine days) and Francis Drake met Queen Elizabeth on his return from sailing around the world on the *Golden Hind*.

Syon is owned by the Dukes of Northumberland who have had possession of the house since 1594 when James I gave it to Henry Percy, Earl of Northumberland. In 1762 the architect and designer Robert Adam was invited to remodel the old Tudor nunnery into a building of classical splendour. Although he worked here for years, the project was never entirely finished. The Great Conservatory was designed by Charles Fowler for the third Duke. In the 18th century Capability Brown remodelled the gardens. In 1874

Northumberland House in central London was demolished and the sixth Duke removed much of the furniture and effects to Syon, in particular the Percy Lion (after a model by Michelangelo) which had stood on the London house for 125 years and now stands proudly above the east front.

Above: A welcome and popular watering hole on the river at Richmond. The roadway in front often floods at high tide leaving parked cars up to their mudguards in the Thames.

Starting Points: Richmond railway station (1A) or Richmond car parks (1B). You could do the route in reverse by parking in the Kew Gardens car park just off Kew Green.

Parking: Richmond has many car parks. There's the official station car park, a multi-storey next to the station, meter parking around Richmond Green, a car park just off the river behind the White Cross Hotel (Friars Lane) and a big one off the A316 in the direction of Twickenham. There is parking around Kew Green and in the Kew Gardens car park.

Public Transport: Many trains visit Richmond from Waterloo — the loop line from Waterloo and back via (among others) Clapham Junction, Putney, Richmond, Twickenham, Kingston and Wimbledon; then there are the trains heading out to Reading and Windsor. Richmond is also one end of the extremely useful North London Line that goes through the north of London all the way to North Woolwich. Richmond is also on the District Line.

Links to Other Paths: The Thames Path from Richmond to Kew links with others mentioned in this book — westward to Kingston (see Route 2); eastward you can continue along the river to Barnes (see Route 4); Richmond Park is easily accessible from the river (see Route 16); the route to Syon Park goes past the bottom end of the Grand Union Canal (see Route 9).

Distance: c5km (3 miles) from the station to Kew; returning via Syon gives a round trip of about 12km (7½ miles).

Map: Explorer 161.

Surfaces and Gradients: Good riverside path — some asphalt, some hardstanding; from Kew Bridge back to Richmond Lock via Syon is all on road.

Roads and Crossings: If you come from the station you have to negotiate the road to the river (not too busy or dangerous); if you cross Kew Bridge, the road to Syon is busy as it is an important thoroughfare; from Syon to Richmond Lock the road is quieter but the section on the A3004 can be busy.

Refreshments: Richmond is blessed with many pubs, cafés and restaurants (the White Cross Hotel is practically the start of the route). Kew Green boasts two excellent pubs (Coach & Horses and Rose & Crown) and in Isleworth, just after Syon Park (where there are tea rooms), there's the riverside London Apprentice.

Route Instructions: 1A. Turn left out of the station and cross the road in front (A307) by the pedestrian crossing. Push your bike through the alleyway and turn left on to Parkshot. Follow the road past Richmond Theatre around the Green to Friars Lane car park (1B) which leads to the river.

2. Turn left if you want to start your trip with a drink at the White Cross Hotel; turn right to take the riverside path to Kew.

3. At Kew Bridge you have a number of options: visit the gardens, return by the route you have just taken or return via Syon Park. If you choose the latter, go over the bridge and turn left.

4. The Thames Path meanders around through gardens

Right: Richmond Lock is half tidal and is the only lock on the Thames controlled by the Port of London Authority.

and houses here. It is quicker to take the road (A315, Brentford High Street) for about two miles.

5. A couple of hundred yards after crossing the Grand Union Canal, on the left, is the shared cyclist/pedestrian entrance to Syon Park.

6. Cycle through the park and turn left on to Park Road.

7. At the fork go left and follow Swan Street and Upper Square to join the A3004 (first South Street, it later becomes the Richmond Road).

8. Just past the college turn left on to Kilmorey Road and turn left again on to what becomes Ranelagh Drive.

9. Cross the river at Richmond half-tidal barrier and rejoin the path on the Surrey side.

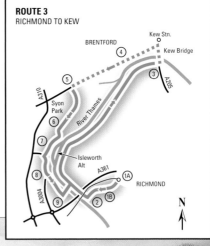

ROUTE 3
RICHMOND TO KEW

BOAT RACE LOOP
(Barnes–Putney Bridge–back to Barnes via Chiswick)

Continuing the Thames Path, this route runs on both sides of the Thames between Barnes, Chiswick and Putney and can be easily linked to Route 3 or, by crossing Putney Bridge, you can cycle into the West End via the King's Road. Short detours from the route allow visits to Chiswick House or Hogarth's House, or a chance to enjoy the pubs and restaurants along Strand-on-the-Green. There are sections of this route that are pedestrian-only and you will have to push your bike. Of particular note is the extremely pretty route from Hammersmith Bridge along Hammersmith Terrace and the Upper and Lower Malls with their fine houses and pubs.

PLACES OF INTEREST

Hammersmith Bridge

Built in 1887 to replace an earlier bridge, this magnificent Victorian bridge is now a protected monument. It was designed by the engineer Sir Joseph Bazalgette (who also created the Thames Embankment) and incorporated the piers and abutments of the previous bridge. The coats of arms at the entrance to the bridge are of the counties of Middlesex and Kent, representing the town of Guildford and the old Metropolitan Board of Works. On the upriver side at the centre of the bridge is a bronze plaque, which commemorates Lt Charles Campbell Wood, RAF of Bloemfontein, South Africa, who at midnight in September 1919 dived into the Thames from this spot to save a drowning woman: sadly he died soon after of injuries sustained in the rescue. In 1939 the bridge was the target of the IRA who tried to blow it up with a bomb, but a passer-by threw it into the river.

Right: **The Thames widens out considerably at Barnes. On the left is Harrods Depository.**

Barnes

Barnes has something of the backwater charm of a small rural town of 30 years ago, yet it is only a few miles from the heart of London. There is still even a village pond and green. The author and dramatist Henry Fielding (1707–54) lived in Milbourne House on Barnes Green. He became a Justice of the Peace, and with his half brother, Sir John Fielding, helped to set up the Bow Street Runners. The composer Gustav Holst lived at 9 The Terrace between 1908–13. The railway bridge was built between 1846–9 of cast iron with vertically ribbed open spandrels by Joseph Locke and J. E. Errington for the London & South Western Railway; this is the oldest remaining bridge below Richmond. Although it is now disused by the railway, it is used as a footpath across the river. The wrought iron bow-string bridge alongside downstream was built in 1891–5.

Chiswick House

Originally a small Palladian-style villa started in 1725 for the Earl of Burlington, with a William Kent-designed garden, inspired by the Italian countryside. The park contains tree-lined avenues, temples, sphinxes, lions, fawns and satyrs plus the great gateway designed by Inigo Jones. This latter structure was given to Burlington by Sir John Soane when its original Chelsea site at Sir Thomas More's house was about to be demolished.

Inspired by taking the Grand Tour of Europe (twice), Burlington decided to make his Italianate villa not as somewhere to live, but as a centre for arts and culture, where

fine paintings, sculptures and good books would live surrounded by witty and erudite conversation. After his death Chiswick House passed through to the Dukes of Devonshire; the fifth Duke demolished much of the Jacobean building in 1764 and instead added a new wing containing living rooms and bedrooms.

Many famous people have stayed or visited here including Alexander Pope, Jonathan Swift, the Duke of Wellington, Blücher, the Tsar of Russia, Queen Victoria and Garibaldi.

Chiswick Bridge

Built in 1933 by A. Dryland and Sir Herbert Baker, the bridge is faced with Portland stone and the central arch has the longest concrete span over the Thames, at almost 46m (150ft). It is the finishing point of the annual University Boat Race between Oxford and Cambridge.

Hogarth's House

A brick-built country house, and the retreat of the painter William Hogarth from 1749 until his death in 1764, after which his wife Jane remained there until her own death. It was turned into a museum in 1909, housing the artist's prints including his best known works. He originally painted in a stable converted to a studio in the garden, now long since gone, though an ancient mulberry tree dating back to his time is still alive today.

Strand-on-the-Green

The towpath runs between this pretty row of mainly 18th century houses — at one time a fishing village — and the Thames on the Chiswick side (left bank). Indeed, at the seasonal autumn and spring high tides the path is often underwater — which accounts for the rise of steps and high front doors on some of the houses. An especial feature of these houses are their charming gardens which seem to flourish all year round. At number 65, the German painter Johann Zoffany (1733–1810) lived between the years 1790–1810. He was a successful court painter and favourite of George III, and was also a founder member of the Royal Academy. Other famous one-time residents include Nancy Mitford, Margaret Kennedy, Geoffrey Household, Jerrard Tickell, Dylan Thomas, Goronwy Rees, Lord Cudlipp and Air Marshal Sir John Slessor.

Two pubs at the far end of the towpath are a welcome sight. The first, the City Barge, was built in 1497 when it was called the Navigators Arms. The name change came in Victorian times because the Lord Mayor of London's barge had its winter moorings here. A few steps further lies the Bull's Head, a 17th century pub at which, tradition has it, during the Civil War Oliver Cromwell met his council but was forced to escape his enemies by way of an underground passage to an islet in the Thames, called in honour of the occasion, Oliver's Eyot.

Starting Points: Barnes Bridge railway station (1A), Barnes railway station (1B), or car park by Chiswick Bridge (9).

Parking: There is parking by Chiswick Bridge and limited roadside parking around Barnes.

Public Transport: South West trains visit Barnes regularly from Waterloo. Barnes Bridge is on the Hounslow line and served less frequently.

Links to Other Paths: Links to Route 3 by continuing from Chiswick Bridge to Kew Bridge.

Distance: Chiswick Bridge to Putney Bridge is c6.5km (4 miles); the round trip is about 13km (8 miles).

Map: Explorer 161.

Surfaces and Gradients: Flat riverside paths.

Roads and Crossings: Some road work along traffic-calmed back roads.

Refreshments: Barnes, Putney, Hammersmith and Chiswick have many pubs and locations for refreshments. Of particular note are the Ship at Mortlake, the White Hart and Bull's Head at Barnes, and the Black Lion, Old Ship and Blue Anchor at Hammersmith.

Route Instructions:

1A. Turn right out of Barnes Bridge station on to the A3003 (The Terrace) and carry on over the mini-roundabout on to the B350 (Lonsdale Road) along the Thames.
or
1B. From Barnes station take the path along the railway line, turn right and follow the road until it joins the B349 (Station Road). Turn left when the B349 joins the A3003 (Barnes High Street) and turn right at the mini-roundabout on to the B350 (Lonsdale Road) along the Thames.

Above: To go round Fulham football ground and reach Hammersmith Bridge you must take to the roads.

2. Continue along the path to Hammersmith Bridge where you can cross to the other side of the river and cut out the Putney end of the route. (Continue from 5 below.)

3. Cross Putney Bridge (where the Oxford and Cambridge boat race starts) and turn left on to the cycle path through the grounds of Fulham Palace.

4. You must join the road to go round Fulham football ground; thereafter it is easier to cycle along the back streets to Hammersmith Bridge (via Stevenage Road, Lysia Street, Woodlawn Road, Crabtree Lane, Rannoch Road, Manbre Road, Winslow Road, Distillery Road, Chancellor's Road and Crisp Road).

5. From Hammersmith Bridge the path follows the river and riverside roads to Barnes Bridge (Lower Mall, Upper Mall, Smith Terrace, Chiswick Mall, Chiswick Lane, Pumping Station Road, Grantham Road, The Promenade). In some areas — especially at the start — you may have to walk your bike due to cycling restrictions.

6. At Church Street just off the A4/A316 roundabout it is worth detouring to visit Chiswick House and Hogarth's House. You can catch the train from nearby Chiswick station.

7. Either rejoin the path on the riverside or take the alley from near Chiswick station; it goes along the line to Barnes Bridge which can be crossed.

8. Go under the railway line and cycle along the road through Dukes Meadows past the sports ground to Chiswick Bridge (where the boat race ends).

9. Cross Chiswick Bridge and join the Thames Path on the Surrey side. Return to Barnes.

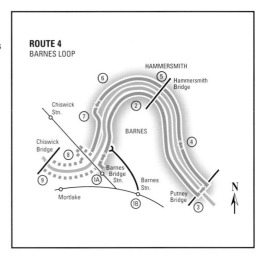

ROUTE 4
BARNES LOOP

WATERLOO TO TOWER BRIDGE

This is not the route for cyclists who want to stretch their legs and pound the pedals: it is a short, gentle cycle ride allowing fantastic views of some of the most historic sights of London — from the new (the London Eye, the South Bank, the new Bankside Tate building) to the ancient (Southwark Cathedral, the rebuilt Globe theatre, the Tower of London). Most is off-road but it certainly isn't without traffic: even on the wettest Sunday morning there are walkers and runners. Make sure you have your cycle locks for this one because you'll spend as much of the time off the bike as on.

PLACES OF INTEREST

Houses of Parliament

Properly called the Palace of Westminster, the first palace was built for Edward the Confessor, then in 1066 his successor, William the Conqueror brought his court here. Although much extended and improved, the palace remained as the premier royal residence until Henry VIII moved to Whitehall Palace in 1512. After the Dissolution of the Monasteries (and all other religious institutions) in 1547 the old Royal Chapel of St Stephen was used as a debating chamber, the members sitting in the choir stalls on the north and south walls with the Speaker presiding over the debates from his chair on the site of the altar. This arrangement continued until 1834 when a great fire destroyed much of the palace, leaving the chapel badly damaged with only the crypt surviving. The only other surviving parts were Westminster Hall, the cloisters and the Jewel Tower.

A purpose-built 'Gothic or Elizabethan style' building was decided on, and local boy Charles Barry won the commission; he in turn asked the Gothic specialist Augustus Pugin to assist him with the project. They worked well together —

Barry drew up the plans and Pugin embellished them. Building began in 1837, and by 1847 the Commons was completed in Perpendicular Gothic style.

Between September 1940 and May 1941 the Houses of Parliament were damaged 11 times by Luftwaffe air raids. The worst damage happened on 10 May 1941 when 500 German aircraft dropped hundreds of incendiary bombs, turning the buildings into an inferno. The House of Commons and Lobby were destroyed. Sir Giles Gilbert Scott was commissioned for the rebuilding (1945–50) and his work is true to the spirit of Barry and Pugin although less elaborately Gothic.

London Eye

Properly termed the British Airways London Eye, this massive 137m (450ft)-high Ferris wheel was erected after initial difficulties in October 1999 in time for the Millennium celebrations although it was not working for the public on the big night. It cost £20 million and weighs 1,500 tonnes. The wheel was designed by husband and wife

Below: **The London Eye.** *A.N.T. Photographic*

team Julia Barfield and David Marks; it is planned to remain here for five years. On a clear day visitors should be able to see seven counties from the top of the wheel.

Big Ben

Properly speaking, this is Victoria Tower and the light above the clock is switched on when Parliament is in session.

A high clock tower was a feature of Barry's design for the new Parliament building but for five years heated arguments followed as to who should make the clock mechanism itself. In 1852 the commission was finally allocated to E. J. Dent and work started, and although he died the following year his commission was continued by his stepson Frederick. By 1854 the clock was

Below: **Big Ben.** *A.N.T. Photographic*

finished but the tower wasn't; this gave the clockmakers five years longer than expected to test and refine the movement. The clock cost £4,080. In 1856 the original 16-ton (15.7-tonne) bell cracked during testing and had to be scrapped, so in 1858 the metal was used in a recasting by George Mears of the Whitechapel Bell Foundry. Pulled by 16 horses, the 2m (7ft)-high, over 13-ton (11.7-tonne) bell was brought through crowded streets on a flat cart to Westminster.

The tower is 103m (336ft) high and 22.8m (75ft) square. On each of the four sides is a clock face 6.6m (22½ft) in diameter and weighing 36 tonnes (40 tons); a minute hand 4.2m (14ft) long made of hollow copper and a 2.7m (9ft)-long gunmetal hour hand. Each minute space is 0.3m (1ft) square and the figures are 0.61m (2ft) high; inside the tower the pendulum is 3.9m (13ft) long and weighs 298kg (658lb). A land line was used to link the clock with the Royal Observatory, Greenwich and the time checked twice a day. It was destroyed in 1940 but never repaired as the clock was so accurate.

The clock became operational on 31 May 1859; the new bell soon cracked but not fatally. In 1913 automatic winding gear was installed. The mechanism was extensively repaired in 1976.

The Globe

The foundations of William Shakespeare's Elizabethan theatre were found during building developments in the 1980s. The American impresario Sam Wannamaker's lifetime ambition was to recreate the Globe in its authentic entirety on the exact site of the original. He was not able to build on the same spot but chose a fine location near the original site. Without his drive and ambition (and that of his daughter Zöe after his death) the Globe would not now stand. Like the original, it is a round wooden structure with a partially thatched roof but open to the air over the stage and auditorium.

The original Globe was built in 1598–9 by Cuthbert and Richard Burbage; it was named after the sign which showed the hero Hercules carrying the world on his shoulders. Many of Shakespeare's greatest plays were performed here. Important patrons could sit on stools on the stage itself, ordinary members of the public paid 1d to stand in the pit, 2d in the gallery and 3d for a seat. The theatre burnt down in 1613 during Henry VIII when a cannon fired during the performance set light to the thatch. However, it was quickly rebuilt the following year with public subscriptions and a royal grant. But by 1642 the Puritans ran England; they thoroughly disapproved of the licentious theatre and closed the Globe (along with all the other playhouses) down. They consolidated this two years later by demolishing the Globe altogether.

Cleopatra's Needle

Halfway between Hungerford and Waterloo Bridges rises a 20.8m (68½ft)-high pink granite obelisk known as Cleopatra's Needle, estimated to weigh 168.7 tonnes. It was placed here in 1878 and within the pedestal are two Victorian time capsules containing items in daily use — including a copy of Bradshaw's Railway Guide plus photographs of the 12 best-looking Englishwomen.

Originally one of a pair of obelisks quarried by Egyptian stonemasons in Aswan around 1500BC, in c1475BC during the Eighteenth Dynasty it was erected at Heliopolis by Tethmosis III who dedicated it to the god Tum. The names of the Egyptian rulers Ramses II and Cleopatra were added at a later date and the hieroglyphs down the sides are a record of their victories and prayers to the gods. In about 12BC it was moved to Alexandria, probably on the orders of the Emperor Augustus. At some point in history the obelisk fell over and was left on the sands until 1819 when it was presented to Britain by Mohammed Ali, Viceroy of Egypt. It was not brought to London for many years because it was considered impossible to move but John Dixon, a local English engineer, worked out a way. However, while being towed on a pontoon to England the obelisk was almost lost during a storm in the Bay of Biscay in which six sailors drowned trying to save it; later burned and broken, it was abandoned

twice because of storms. It finally reached London in January 1878 almost 16 months after leaving Alexandria. It is flanked by two bronze sphinxes by G. J. Vuillamy which still show the bomb damage caused during World War 1. Its twin is in Central Park, New York.

Tower Bridge

Technically a bascule bridge, this most distinctive feature of London is a Victorian Gothic masterpiece designed by Sir Horace Jones and Sir John Wolfe Barry. It took over a million pounds and eight years to build and was opened by Edward, Prince of Wales (later Edward VII) in 1894.

The bridge allows ships up to 9,072 tonnes (10,000 tons) to pass underneath at high tide. When London was a thriving port it used to open up to five times a day — now it is quite unusual to see the bridge open. A lift on either shore side takes pedestrians up to the footbridge; alternatively almost 300 stairs can be climbed to the top. Open access to the footbridge was closed in 1910 due to the number of suicides, but it has now reopened to the public as a glazed-in walkway.

Waterloo Bridge

The present bridge was built in 1937–42, but not officially opened until after the war. It is of cantilever reinforced concrete box girders by Rendel, Palmer & Tritton. Sir Giles Gilbert Scott was the architect.

Hungerford Railway Bridge

Also known as Charing Cross Bridge. Built for the South Eastern Railway by Sir John Hawkshaw and completed in 1864, it is a nine-span wrought iron lattice girder bridge with a footbridge running parallel alongside. The footbridge resounds to the din of thousands of commuters every working day during rush hour, which becomes a thundering roar when a train clatters in or out of Charing Cross station.

Blackfriars Railway Bridge

Built for the London, Chatham & Dover Railway in 1862–4 by Joseph H. Cubitt and F. T. Turner. Massive pylons support abutments bearing the railway's insignia and huge Romanesque cast iron columns carry the wrought iron lattice girder bridge. It is now unused.

Blackfriars Bridge

Built in 1860–9 by Joseph H. Cubitt and H. Carr to replace an earlier bridge. Granite piers support five wrought iron arches faced with cast iron. It was opened by Queen Victoria on the same day as Holborn Viaduct — not a happy day as she and her servant John Brown were hissed at by the crowds in the Strand.

HMS *Belfast*

This seven-decked Royal Navy cruiser lies moored at Symon's Wharf. She has had a distinguished past before becoming a floating museum. She served with the Russian convoys in World War 2, supported the Normandy landings, fought in the battle which sank the *Scharnhorst* and at one time did a tour in the Far East and fought in the Korean War. The *Belfast* is kept as a working RN ship as far as possible.

Bankside Power Station

Now being rebuilt to house the new annexe of the Tate art gallery, Bankside was carefully designed by Sir Giles Gilbert Scott so as not to be an eyesore when looking south from the City. The plant was not installed until 1963 and for most of its life used only one oil-fired turbo alternator. The station was closed in 1981 and the building's future was in considerable doubt until the Tate took it.

Starting Points: Waterloo station (1A), South Bank car parks (1B), Waterloo Bridge (1C).

Parking: Various car parks along the South Bank; there's parking on Waterloo Bridge at weekends and some meter parking at the back of Waterloo station.

Public Transport: Trains to Waterloo station from all over the south of England and France via the Eurostar!

Links to Other Paths: Cycle along the river to Westminster Bridge; negotiate Parliament Square, turn left on to Great George Street to join Birdcage Walk and Route 22. Continue over Tower Bridge for Route 6 and continue on to Greenwich via Route 7.

Below: HMS *Belfast. A.N.T. Photographic*

ROUTE 5
WATERLOO TO TOWER BRIDGE

Waterloo Bridge — Blackfriars Bridge — Southwark Bridge — London Bridge — Tower Bridge

1C

2 — 1B — 1A — Waterloo Stn. — Southwark Cathedral — 3

N

Distance: A short 7km (4½ miles) round trip.

Map: Explorer 173.

Surfaces and Gradients: Flat roads or riverside paths.

Roads and Crossings: Most of the route is on shared paths or gentle roads. Crossing Tower Bridge by road can be tricky.

Refreshments: There are many places to eat and drink in this area and, surprisingly, not always at ridiculous prices, including the National Theatre and the Anchor on Bankside that dates from 1750.

Route Instructions: 1A. It's best to walk to the South Bank from Waterloo station.
or
1B. You can take the taxi road to York Road, crossing over to Chichester Street and Belvedere Road, and the South Bank car parking.
or
1C. From Waterloo Bridge either circle the roundabout and take Concert Hall approach, or access via Stamford Street and Cornwall Road.

2. From the side of the Old County Hall and the London Eye, cycle east along the river. The bridges have underpasses and you have to cycle on the road around Southwark Cathedral. There are a number of cycling restyrictions on the route: make sure you dismount as necessary.

3. At Tower Bridge you can either retrace your steps, cross to St Katharine's Docks (see Route 6) or continue on the south bank of the Thames to Greenwich (see Route 7).

Above: London is at long last trying to make the most of its wonderful river by promoting the astonishing range of sights — all best seen from the advantage of a bike!

Left: Houses of Parliament.
Nick Lerwill

TOWER BRIDGE TO LIMEHOUSE BASIN

(and on to Greenwich via the north bank)

This is not really a traffic-free route at all, but it's worthy of inclusion in this book because it is a calm route (especially on a Sunday morning) that links well with Canary Wharf, the Isle of Dogs and the Regent's Canal. There's a great deal of the docklands regeneration to see on this route and although the riverside path is often reserved for pedestrians, it's well worth the effort.

PLACES OF INTEREST

St Katharine's Dock

This 9.3ha (23-acre) site was the first area to be developed as part of the regeneration of the London docks and served to show how docklands could be transformed into an attractive and prosperous region. Designed originally by Thomas Telford and Philip Hardwick, the project took 2½ years and opened in 1828 on the site of the Royal Foundation of St Katharine founded in 1148 for the sick and infirm by Matilda, wife of King Stephen. The dock was built at a cost of £1,352,752 and over 11,000 people were evicted without compensation from 1,033 homes to make way for the project. The basin comprises 0.6ha (1.5 acres) of water and two irregularly shaped docks of 1.6ha (4 acres) each.

St Katharine's was the furthest upstream of the old London docks; furthermore, it was the first to have warehouses built directly on to the waterfront so that goods could be lifted by crane straight from the ship's hold into the warehouse. The dock, however, was never as successful as it should have been as the entrance lock was too small for contemporary ships even by the time it opened, so barges became intermediaries between the warehouses and the shipping. With the advent of steamships in the second half of the 19th century business rapidly declined and in 1940 the warehouses around the East Dock were destroyed by bombing as well as the imposing Dock Offices on the West Basin. St Katharine's was finally closed for good in 1968. Then in 1969 the GLC (having bought the site from the Port of London Authority for £1.5 million), determined to rejuvenate the area with the restoration of the warehouses and docks and the creation of a marina, held a competition for the project. This was won by Taylor Woodrow who were awarded a 125-year lease. The first job was to demolish the great dock walls which revealed the expanse of water; however, in an act of architectural vandalism all but one of the magnificent warehouses were demolished. The dock has become a thriving and prosperous area and a much sought-after address.

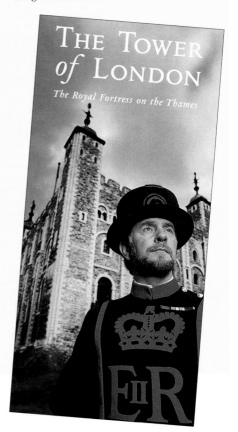

THE TOWER of LONDON

The Royal Fortress on the Thames

Right: The Tower of London is justly one of the most popular visitor attractions in the country.

Wapping

Wapping itself was once the heart of London's docklands and as a result was intimately linked with the successes and losses of British shipping. For centuries this was an area populated by the poor whose living depended on the river and sea — chandlers, shipwrights, sailors, lightermen and their families. In fact, until the 18th century it was actually illegal to land any foreign cargo upstream of the Tower except at specified quays in the Pool of London. However, due to the huge increase in cargo and shipping and the subsequent thieving on a massive scale, around the turn of the 19th century secure docks were built to protect the valuable cargoes. Huge areas of Wapping were taken by the new developments and thousands lost their homes. Four great basins were built surrounded by accompanying wharves and warehouses and encircled by intimidating walls: the Western Dock (1805); the Eastern Dock (1828); Shadwell Old Basin (1831) and Shadwell New Basin (1858). By 1880 Wapping Docks were hugely prosperous, but outside their secure walls the people were poor, overcrowded and the area notorious for crime, poverty and suffering. Even worse was to come during the bombing raids of World War 2 when much of the docks area was reduced to rubble by the Luftwaffe. The area went into social and economic decline until the building redevelopments started in the latter half of the 20th century.

Wapping High Street

Linking Wapping Pier Head (the original 1805 entrance for London Docks) to Shadwell Basin, this was once a thriving dockland area of wharves and warehouses. The area went into seemingly terminal decline after the damage of the wartime Luftwaffe raids although its remaining historic buildings — including terraces of 18th century houses — now form a conservation area. However, with its proximity to the City and to the new docklands developments, it has now become an area of swanky loft apartments and smart offices behind the almost continuous line of high warehouse walls. On the High Street are such notable buildings as Wapping River Police station, which is on the site of the first river police station of 1798, and Wapping Underground station, the end point for the first underwater tunnel to carry public traffic the world had seen. Built by Sir Marc Brunel, assisted by his illustrious son Isambard Kingdom Brunel, the Thames Tunnel (built 1825–43) crosses the river from Rotherhithe to Wapping.

Starting Points: Tower Bridge (1A) from Waterloo via Route 5, Fenchurch Street station (1B).

Parking: There's parking at Tower Gateway, Ensign Street, off the A1203 and over Tower Bridge on Shad Thames.

Public Transport: Rail services to Fenchurch Street station.

Links to Other Paths: Route 5 (back to Waterloo), Route 7 south of the river (together 6 and 7 can be joined to make a round trip to and from Greenwich but they both involve cycling along the road), Route 12 (Regent's Canal circuit).

Distance: c2.5km (1½ miles) to Limehouse Basin, c6km to the Greenwich foot tunnel, c14km (9 miles) round trip going back via the southern route (see Route 7).

Map: Explorer 173.

Surfaces and Gradients: Flat as a pancake; mainly road with some asphalt or paved pathway.

Roads and Crossings: Much of this route is on the road, and from Limehouse it is easy to continue cycling down to the Greenwich foot tunnel at the bottom of the Isle of Dogs. The route follows gentle roads, but getting to St Katharine's Dock from Fenchurch Street station involves crossing busy streets.

Refreshments: All along the route there are splendid old pubs — starting with the timber-framed Charles Dickens Inn in St Katharine's Dock (inside it is part of the otherwise demolished 'G' warehouse dating back to the first decade of the 19th century); the Prospect of Whitby is further on near Shadwell Basin.

Route Instructions: 1A. On Tower Bridge there are stairs to the riverside path.
or
1B. Turn left out of Fenchurch Street station and join Mark Lane. Turn left on to Great Tower Street and subsequently on to Byward Street. Continue along Tower Hill, crossing the road. Walk alongside the Tower and join the riverside path.

2. Walk past the Tower Hotel, through St Katharine's Dock, and join St Katharine's Way.

3. This leads to Wapping High Street . . .

4. . . from which one turns into Wapping Wall. Go past the Prospect of Whitby . . .

5. . . . .and either push your bike along the river to Narrow Street or cycle along a short stretch of the A1203 (Ratcliff Highway) . . .

6. . . . .on to Limehouse Basin. Here you can join the Paddington Arm of the Grand Union Canal (see Routes 9 and 10) or continue on to Canary Wharf.

7. If you continue, and wish to make a circuit back to Tower Bridge, from Westferry Circus at the base of Canary Wharf follow Westferry Road to Island Gardens DLR station where the Greenwich Foot Tunnel will take you under the river and link with Route 7.

Right: The creation of St Katharine's Marina was an obvious move for the developers, Taylor Woodrow.

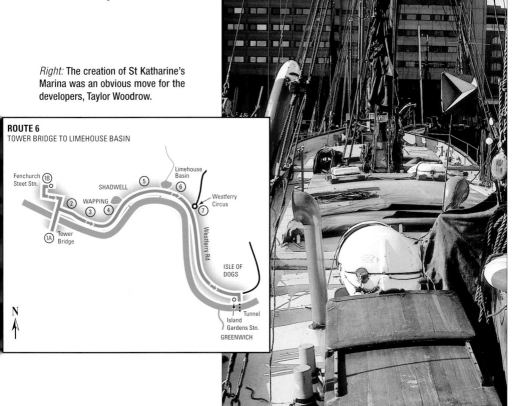

ROUTE 6
TOWER BRIDGE TO LIMEHOUSE BASIN

Fenchurch Steet Stn. (1B)
SHADWELL
Limehouse Basin
5
6
Westferry Circus
2 WAPPING
3 4
7
Westferry Rd
(1A) Tower Bridge

ISLE OF DOGS

Tunnel
Island Gardens Stn.
GREENWICH

N

London Docklands Cycle Routes

1997

🏛London Docklands

TOWER BRIDGE TO
GREENWICH (South Bank route)

Instead of crossing Tower Bridge as in the previous route, continue along the south bank of the river past what used to be the Surrey Commercial Docks — now only represented by Greenland Dock — through Deptford to Greenwich. Another wonderful riverside route, dominated by views of Canary Wharf, it can be combined with Route 6 to provide a brilliant view of the Docklands regeneration.

PLACES OF INTEREST

Surrey Commercial Docks

Two miles east of London Bridge on the south bank of the Thames lie the old Surrey Commercial Docks. At their peak they covered 121ha (300 acres), comprised nine docks, six timber ponds and canals of 5.6km (3.5 miles), all belonging to four different companies, and were the only enclosed docks on the southern side of the Thames. Surrey Docks evolved around the old Howland Great Wet Dock (1696). Renamed Greenland Dock in 1763 it was associated with the whaling trade until that declined and trade turned to softwood from the Baltic and Scandinavia. At one time Surrey Docks were the largest timber handling docks in Europe.

The first dock was formed from the navigable cut dug by the Surrey Canal Company with the intention of linking Rotherhithe to Epsom and then the Wey Navigation to bring local market garden produce to the centre of London. But by 1807 the cut was being transformed into the Grand Surrey Basin for harbouring shipping. Also in 1807 the Commercial Dock Company constructed its dock; then in 1809 the Baltic Dock was built; in 1811, East Country Dock; in 1860, Albion Dock; in 1876, Canada Dock; then finally in 1926,

Quebec Dock. During the war the docks suffered massive bomb damage from the Luftwaffe, but the South Dock was pumped dry and used for the construction of some of the concrete caissons for Mulberry Harbour which were floated over the Channel for the D-Day landings. Closed since 1969, the docks have been filled in and used for housing and redevelopment.

Above: London Docklands quickly realised the cycling potential of their development and have done a lot to encourage cyclists.

Below: The glass dome on the Isle of Dogs is the terminal for the Victorian foot-tunnel under the Thames. Canary Wharf tower is on the left in the distance.

Above: Another view of the Isle of Dogs from Greenwich landing stage.

ROUTE 7
TOWER BRIDGE TO GREENWICH

Starting Points: Tower Bridge (1A) from Waterloo via Route 5; London Bridge station (1B).

Parking: There's a car park at Curlew Street and street parking in the area.

Public Transport: Rail services to London Bridge.

Links to Other Paths: This links with Routes 5 and 6 to produce a c20km (12½-mile) route from Waterloo to Greenwich and back. Links at Greenwich with Routes 8 and 27.

Distance: c12km (7½-mile) round trip — a little more if you return using Route 6.

Map: Explorer 173.

Surfaces and Gradients: No gradients to speak of; surfaces are good but be wary of cobblestones in the rain and the ubiquitous glass shards that can be found near most of the many pubs en route.

Roads and Crossings: Unfortunately, much of this route is on roads, but they are quiet ones. The main problem is at the

Deptford end where it is usually quicker to take to the busy A200 (Evelyn Street and Creek Road).

Refreshments: Many tempting places on the first half-mile from Tower Bridge, and at Greenwich; there are also pubs and cafes scattered around the rest of the route.

Route Instructions: 1A. From Route 5 simply go under Tower Bridge and on to Shad Thames.
or
1B. From London Bridge station head to the river either over the Tooley Street footbridge or by turning left out of Station Approach on to the A3 (High Street) and then turning right on to Bedale Street. Follow this road round to the right and pass in front of Southwark Cathedral, joining the Thames Path.

2. Follow the path along the river — Shad Thames, Bermondsey Wall, through King's Stairs Gardens and Rotherhithe Street.

3. The Rotherhithe Peninsula has made the most of its reclaimed docklands (the Surrey Commercial Docks mentioned above) and you can find here sports grounds, a nature reserve, woodlands — and, of course, the Surrey Docks Farm which is definitely worth a detour if you're with small children. An interesting deviation from the river route is to turn onto Albion Way and ride the shared pedestrian/cycle path to Canada Water. From here cross the Surrey Quays Retail Area to reach Greenland Dock's south-westerly extremity.

4. From the farm take Odessa Street then cross Greenland Dock along Southsea Street. The Greenland Dock development is worth a look — particularly the entrance lock and hydraulics — before heading off over the South Dock swing bridge, one of the Surrey Dock's oldest surviving features, towards Deptford.

5. The quickest way to Greenwich from here is by road — turn right on to Plough Way and then left on to the B206 (Grove Street) that joins the busy A200 (Evelyn Street). Alternatively, follow the Thames Path signs for a more interesting but more circuitous path.

6. Evelyn Street becomes Creek Road and enters Greenwich crossing Deptford Creek.

7. The Victorian foot tunnel that allows you to cross to the Isle of Dogs joins Routes 6 and 7. You can also extend your route now to the Barrier by following Route 8.

Below: **Albion Way is a shared cycle/ pedestrian path from the Thames to Canada Water.**

Right: **Greenland Dock.**

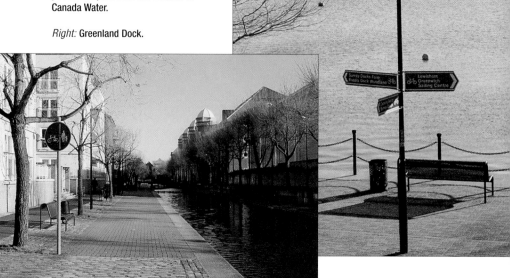

GREENWICH TO THE BARRIER

The route from Greenwich to the Barrier allows spectacular views of the old, in the form of the Royal Naval College and maritime Greenwich, and the new — the Millennium Dome and the Thames Barrier. At the start, on the river in Greenwich, are two famous ships — the Cutty Sark and Francis Chichester's Gipsy Moth IV. On the other bank you have good views of the Isle of Dogs and, from the café at the Barrier, there's a wonderful modern ley line as you see Barrier, Dome and Canary Wharf aligned.

PLACES OF INTEREST

The Dome

Sitting neatly on the south bank in a large loop of the Thames is the Millennium Dome, centre of Britain's Millennium festivities and the largest domed structure in the world. The 52.6ha (130-acre) site is part of a former gas works which was bought in 1997 by English Partnerships, a government regeneration agency. On the remaining 48ha (119 acres) will be built the environmentally sound Millennium Village incorporating 1,400 social and private housing, schools and community buildings ready for 2000, with more development planned for later years.

The initial budget for the Dome was a massive £758 million, and the design and building is a collaboration between the exhibition designer Imagination, architect Richard Rogers Partnership and engineer Buro Happold. For the Millennium year the Dome will celebrate the best of British ideas, culture and technology within 12 time zones.

The Dome is 350m (1,148ft) in diameter and 50m (164ft) high at the central point; the 10m (32.8ft)-high perimeter wall is 1km (0.6 miles) in circumference. The entire Dome is suspended from 12 yellow 100m (328ft) steel 50-tonne masts, each raked back at 17° and anchored by two twin-cable back stays. The support stays for the building itself descend from special cable anchorage points in the top 2m (6.5ft) of the masts, to points in the centre and back of the Dome. The whole is held in place by over 70km (43 miles) of high strength cable. The top of each mast is connected to the building below via a series of 26 steel cables measuring up to 40mm (1.7in) in diameter. The construction required more than 2,000 workers. The Dome itself is made of a translucent weather-proof fabric and able to accommodate 50,000 visitors who enter through six gateways. A second mezzanine level contains shops, food and drink retailers.

Thames Barrier

Central London last flooded in 1928 when 14 people drowned, but it has come close

Below: **A view of the Millennium Dome.**

Above: **Close-up of one of the Thames Barrier piers — an absolutely remarkable feat of engineering.**

Queen in May 1984, this is a major part of the flood defences of London, used to protect the city from the sea's rising water levels and tidal surges. UK tax payers raised 75% of the cost and the rest was raised through London rates. In its first 12 operating years the Barrier has been closed 29 times to protect London from flooding, as well as being closed regularly for testing. Dangerous conditions can be forecast up to two days in advance — the Barrier Controller decides to close when the predicted incoming tide height coupled with analysis from the Barrier's computers forecast dangerous conditions.

The Barrier takes 30 minutes to close and is raised three to four hours before the peak of the incoming tidal surge. The Port of London Authority is informed and in turn it warns shipping. Red 'X' lights on the Barrier give the visible warning. The Barrier itself spans the 520m Woolwich Reach stretch of the Thames and consists of 10 separate moveable gates which pivot from their concrete piers and abutments. Like an iceberg, much of its bulk is hidden under the waterline. Each of the four main gates weighs 3,700 tonnes and stands as high as a five-storey building. Over 50 staff operate and maintain the Barrier.

on more recent occasions. Traditionally, London has been protected by raising bankside defences and building ever higher walls, but these alone are insufficient, so the decision was taken to build a barrier across the Thames. Built by the Environment Agency and opened by the

Starting Points: Greenwich railway station (1A), parking at Greenwich (1B) or at the Barrier itself (6) if you want to do the route in reverse.

Parking: There are car parks and meter parking in Greenwich (Park Row is convenient but busy) and a car park at the Barrier.

Public Transport: Greenwich railway station is served by trains from Waterloo East, Cannon Street and London Bridge. Unfortunately, the splendid new Jubilee Line does not carry bicycles.

Links to Other Paths: Cross by the Greenwich foot tunnel to reach the Isle of Dogs. Cycle along Westferry Road, Bow Street and Scott Street to reach the

Below: **The huge Thames Barrier is lowered into place whenever a high tide threatens to flood London.**

Limehouse Cut (Route 12). Route 27 follows the river path in part.

Distance: c5km (3 miles) each way giving a 9–10km (c6 miles) round trip.

Map: Explorer 162.

Surfaces and Gradients: Flat riverside path and road.

Roads and Crossings: The road from the station is busy. After this, the major difficulty is the A102 Blackwall Tunnel approach road but this can be crossed by a footbridge. If you return to Greenwich along the A206 be very careful, it's busy.

Refreshments: Greenwich is full of pubs and other places to find refreshments, the Trafalgar by the Royal Naval College providing particularly good value. At the Barrier there is a café.

Route Instructions: 1A. From the station turn left on to the A206 (Greenwich High Road) and follow the road around on to Greenwich Church Street which leads down to the river.

2. Make your way along the river from Greenwich Pier, in front of the Royal Naval College to the Trafalgar pub.

Below: **Greenwich river front.**

or

1B. From Park Row car park join the route by the Trafalgar pub.

3. From the Trafalgar follow the Thames Path . . .

4. . . . and cross the A102 by the footbridge.

5. Follow Dreadnought Street, turn left on to Blackwall Lane and then right on to River Way.

6. Follow the path to the Barrier.

7. Either return to your car, retrace your steps to Greenwich or take Harden's Manor Way back to the A206 (Woolwich Road). Turn right and follow the A206 to Greenwich.

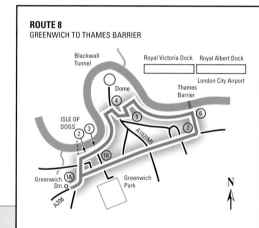

ROUTE 8
GREENWICH TO THAMES BARRIER

Grand Union Canal

The Grand Union Canal is actually at least eight canal systems integrated to form a continuous waterway linking the great port and city of London to the heartland of manufacturing England — specifically Birmingham, Leicester and Nottingham. Originally, all the different systems were owned and maintained by separate companies and until the building of the Grand Junction Canal at the beginning of the 18th century all cargo wound down from the Midlands to London via Coventry and Oxford and from there for the last 161km (100 miles) by lighter to Brentford. The Grand Junction Canal cut a direct route between Braunton (near Oxford) and Brentford in west London and in the process trimmed 96.5km (60 miles) off the distance. Furthermore, the builders of the Grand Junction dug their canal wider than existing systems to enable bigger, 63.5-tonne (70-ton) barges to navigate the waterways. Unfortunately, the other companies could not afford to follow suit and the ambition of the scheme failed to some extent. The Grand Junction, however, brought prosperity to the towns it passed through and encou-

raged the cutting of more canalways. The first Grand Union Canal was opened in 1814 to link the Grand Junction to the Leicestershire and Nottinghamshire canals. Then, in 1820 the Regent's Canal Company opened a new route from the Grand Junction's Paddington arm (Little Venice) to Limehouse for the proposed new docks. The various systems were united as the Grand Union Canal Company in 1929 and in 1932 the government ploughed over a million pounds into a modernisation scheme for the entire system, including widening locks and dredging, but inevitably the money ran out and the project was unfinished. Commerce swapped to the quicker roads and railways and the Grand Union along with other British canals declined into disuse. In 1948, along with all the other waterways, it was taken over by the British Transport Commission, and then again in 1963 by the British Waterways Board. However, life is coming back to the canals as local authorities and conservation groups realise their invaluable potential for recreation and urban renewal and money is again being spent on these wonderful waterways.

Below: The Paddington Arm of the Grand Union Canal.

GRAND UNION CANAL — BRENTFORD TO SLOUGH

This route runs from the western junction of the Thames and the Grand Union at Brentford along the Slough Arm that starts at Cowley Peachey Junction. You can stop at the boundary of Greater London (near Iver) or continue on to Slough and, very easily although by road, to Windsor. Alternatively, some way before then, you can make a circuit of Osterley.

PLACES OF INTEREST

Brentford

Brentford was an important early crossing point of the Thames as well as being on the main road west out of London. There was a Battle of Brentford in 1016 between Edmund Ironside, King of England, and Canute. This event was commemorated with the erection of a granite column in Ferry Lane in 1909. In 1642 another battle was fought here during the Civil War between the Royalists and Parliamentarians. Unfortunately, much of the older buildings of the town have been destroyed and there has been considerable nondescript redevelopment instead.

Kew Steam Museum

The tall tower and a few steam pumping engines are all that remain of the original buildings although there are other steam exhibits inside as well. The museum is organised by the Kew Bridge Engine Trust formed to preserve the remaining machinery.

Osterley House

Originally Osterley manor house, the building began in 1577 as the country retreat for the hugely wealthy city financier Sir Thomas Gresham who occasionally entertained Elizabeth I here. After his death the estate changed hands many times until it was bought in 1711 by Sir Francis Child, an extremely wealthy City banker. He never lived there himself and the estate passed successively to his sons and grandsons. The latter, Francis and Robert, extensively rebuilt the house leaving only the original four corner towers standing. In 1762 Robert Adam got to work and personally oversaw all the interior detail including the design of the furniture. He was also responsible for the six-columned portico. Through inheritance the estate became the property of the Earls of Jersey and in 1923 the 9th Earl gave the entire estate to the National Trust to ensure its future, although the Department of the Environment (to which it is leased) is responsible for the maintenance, and the Victoria and Albert Museum is responsible for the administration.

The parkland around the house contains three long lakes and many exotic trees which were planted 200 years ago. Behind the house and hidden by trees is a Doric Temple of Pan by John James c1720 and a semi-circular orangery designed by Robert Adam. The remarkable trees and fine meadowland where herds of cattle graze and horses gallop provide a view of ancient Middlesex. This impression is shattered to the north part of the park where the M4 cuts through part of the estate.

Above: Brentford Lock at the start of the Grand Union Canal.

Starting Points: Brentford railway station (1A), Syon Park (1B), or wherever you park in Brentford.

Parking: There is parking in Brentford but why not combine your cycling with a visit to Syon Park located a few minutes away (see Route 3) and make use of the car park?

Public Transport: Brentford railway station is on the Hounslow line from Waterloo and served twice an hour (once on Sundays).

Links to Other Paths: Links to Routes 3, 10 and 11.

Distance: c25km (c16 miles) to Slough, c30km (c19 miles) to Windsor.

Maps: Explorer 161, Landranger 175 and 176.

Surfaces and Gradients: Good towpath and roads, slight incline past Osterley Locks.

Roads and Crossings: Small amount of quite busy road from starting points. If you continue to Windsor the section from Slough is quite busy but you can always return to Waterloo from Windsor and Eton Riverside station.

Refreshments: Pubs and cafés at Brentford, along the canal and in Iver, Slough, Eton and Windsor.

Route Instructions: 1A. Turn left on to the A3002 (Boston Manor Road) and follow it until it joins the A315 (High Street).

or

1B. See Route 5 for directions from Syon.

2. Turn right and follow the A315 for less than half a mile.

3. Join the canal at Brentford Lock.

4. The route up the canal is easy to follow as it changes sides only once — at Gallows Bridge (surprisingly steep) — until Cowley Peachey Junction.

5. If you want, you can leave the route at Osterley Lock or Windmill Bridge (take the B454, Windmill Lane), turn right into Jersey Road and then right again into Osterley Park. When you reach the T-junction at Osterley Lane turn left and continue on to the A4127 (Tentflow Lane). Turn right and this takes you back to Windmill Bridge; cross the railway line and cycle in to Osterley Park.

6. Just make sure you don't turn right at Bull's Bridge and join the Paddington Arm.

7. Cross the canal at Cowley Peachey Junction and continue as far west as you want, returning by cycle or train (Iver, Langley and Slough all have stations), or continue from Slough to Windsor by road.

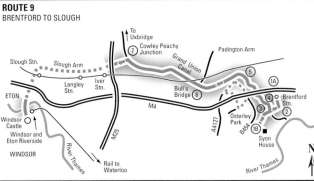

ROUTE 9
BRENTFORD TO SLOUGH

Left: The canal rises gently as it goes past Osterley.

GRAND UNION CANAL — COWLEY PEACHEY JUNCTION NORTHWARD

This route covers the northern reaches of the Grand Union, which affords access northward to Watford, Berkhamsted and, ultimately, Birmingham. The route from Brentford up to, say, Tring makes an entertaining day out, with plenty of wildlife and countryside. But beware: during the fishing season you will share the path with lots of people with extraordinarily long rods (why they don't buy smaller ones and go to the other bank always amazes me). These rods and various other bits of angling impedimenta need to be negotiated with care.

PLACES OF INTEREST

Cowley-Peachey Junction
The Grand Union canal splits at Cowley-Peachy Junction, with the Slough arm and a stretch to the west. From Cowley the land rises uphill to the Chiltern Hills through the Colne Valley. At the beginning of the 19th century a daily passenger and mail service ran between Cowley and Paddington along the Grand Junction Canal. The 'Paddington Packet Boat' was pulled by four horses along the 24km (15-mile) stretch of canal and as the Royal Mail it took precedence over all other water traffic so that it could run on time. At Cowley there remains the Paddington Packet Boat Inn as a reminder of the long-defunct service.

Uxbridge
Once an important market town and coaching post on the road between Oxford and London, it was originally called Wxebridge after the local Saxon tribe called the Wixan. Uxbridge developed as the local market centre during the 12th century and by 1600 was the most important corn market for west Middlesex and south Buckinghamshire, much of the grain being milled along the River Colne. Corn remained the staple resource of Uxbridge between 1790 and 1840, bringing great prosperity to the community. The opening of the Grand Junction Canal in 1805 brought even more trade. In the 1830s an average of 40 coaches posted through Uxbridge every day; this was reduced in 1838 when the Great Western Railway (just under 4.8km [3 miles] away) took much of the trade. This coupled with the reduction in local corn growing reduced the prosperity of the town. By 1907 Uxbridge's central position in the transport network was demonstrated by its four railway termini — the Great Western Railway, 1856; the Metropolitan Railway, 1904; another GWR branch line in 1907; and London United Tramways in 1904.

Starting Points: Brentford (1A), West Drayton station (1B), or around Cowley.

Parking: There is parking in Brentford and around Cowley.

Public Transport: Brentford railway station is on the Hounslow line from Waterloo and is served twice an hour (once on Sundays). West Drayton is on the Slough line out of Paddington and served half-hourly.

Links to Other Paths: Links to Routes 3, 9, and 11.

Distance: 48km (30 miles) to Marsworth Junction, 35km (22 miles) or so to Berkhamsted.

Maps: Explorer 161; Landranger 176 and 166.

Surfaces and Gradients: Good towpath and roads; some slight inclines at locks.

Roads and Crossings: Small amount of quite busy road from Brentford starting point. If you return via rail there will be short road sections from the canal to the station.

Refreshments: Pubs and cafés at Brentford, along the canal and in Uxbridge, Watford, Hemel Hempstead and Berkhamsted.

Route Instructions:1A. Follow the instructions for Route 9.
or
1B. Turn right on to the High Street. Join the canal on the other side of bridge 192 and turn left.

2. Follow the canal northward as far as you want, changing sides a number of times at bridges 188 (Cowley Lock), 184 (Uxbridge Lock), 182 (Denham), 166 (Cassiobury Park Locks), 163 (just before Lady Capel's Lock), 158 (Kings Langley Lock), 155 (before Apsley), 154 (near Apsley station), 153 (Apsley Yard), 144 (before Berkhamsted), etc.

3. Railway return to Euston is accomplished from Tring, Berkhamsted, Boxmoor or Apsley.

Above: Bull's Bridge.

Below: Urban to start with, the Grand Union becomes more rural on its way into Hertfordshire

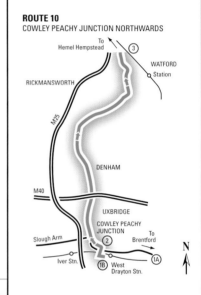

ROUTE 10
COWLEY PEACHY JUNCTION NORTHWARDS

GRAND UNION CANAL —
THE PADDINGTON ARM
(Bull's Bridge to Little Venice)

This is an excellent route into the west of London, giving easy access to Regent's Park Zoo, Portobello Road market (open on Saturdays; take the B450, Ladbroke Grove, by crossing Kensal Green Bridge just after Kensal Green Cemetery, and turn left after the A40 flyover at Elgin Crescent), and the West End. On the canal you speed over stationary traffic coming up to Hangar Lane courtesy of a splendid aqueduct rebuilt recently by Balfour Beatty. The quiet suburbia of Horsenden Hill and Perivale Wood with parkland and wildlife contrasts starkly with the roar of traffic on the North Circular.

PLACES OF INTEREST

Little Venice
This picturesque area of London is so-called after the canal which gives the area its charm and on which many colourful houseboats bob. It lies at the junction of the Regent's and Grand Junction Canals. However, it seems that it was only christened Little Venice some time after the last war although both Byron and Browning had remarked on the likeness. The nearby Rembrandt Gardens were named in 1975 to mark the 700th anniversary of the founding of Amsterdam.

Zoological Gardens
London Zoo is the public face of the Zoological Society of London, and is located in part of Regent's Park in an area originally laid out by Decimus Burton. The Society was founded in April 1826 for the study of animal physiology and the advancement of knowledge about animals. In this capacity it has become a major centre for animal study and research; many of its discussions are aired in the Society's main scientific publication *The Journal of Zoology*. The zoo (although not actually dubbed a 'zoo' until a music hall song gave it the appellation in 1867) opened its gates to Fellows of the Society in 1827 and for a fascinated and enthusiastic public one year later. At this time the main animal attractions included monkeys, bears, kangaroos, llamas and zebras. In 1830 the royal menagerie previously housed at Windsor joined the collection, and then from 1832–4 the exotic animals from the Tower of London were brought here also — these included an Indian elephant and lots of snakes. The zoo can boast a number of 'firsts': the first reptile house in the world opened in 1843; the first aquarium in 1853; and the first insect house in 1881. Each time a new exotic animal arrived it caused a sensation: a chimpanzee in 1835, four giraffes in 1836, in 1840 a pair of lions (which sadly quickly died), a pair of bison in 1847, a hippo in 1850 and an orang-utan the following year, a giant ant-eater in 1853, a sealion in 1856 and two African elephants in 1867.

During World War 2, amid worries of rationing and invasion, most of the dangerous animals were killed, but a few were reprieved and sent instead to Ireland.

Right: The Paddington Arm of the Grand Union enters a tunnel shortly after Little Venice.

After the war the collection was reconstructed and in 1958 the first giant panda — Chi-Chi — arrived. Many of the buildings and animal enclosures have become listed buildings, in particular the Snowdon Aviary (1963–4). The zoo suffered a period of serious economic decline in the 1970s and 1980s but since a thorough restructuring and wholesale alteration of the animal collection it has become one of the principal tourist attractions in London.

Right: **The canal crosses the busy North Circular road by a recently refurbished aqueduct.**

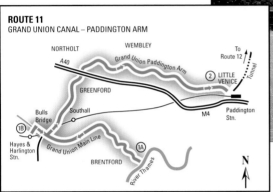

ROUTE 11
GRAND UNION CANAL – PADDINGTON ARM

NORTHOLT
WEMBLEY
A40
Grand Union Paddington Arm
To Route 12
② LITTLE VENICE
Tunnel
GREENFORD
Bulls Bridge
Southall
Grand Union Main Line
M4
Paddington Stn.
①B
Hayes & Harlington Stn.
①A
BRENTFORD
River Thames
N

end depending on the final destination.

Refreshments: Pubs on the canal (although there is little on the canal banks until you reach Alperton). Coffee at Little Venice.

Route Instructions: 1A. From Brentford follow the instructions for Route 11, turning right on to the Paddington Arm of the Grand Union at Bull's Bridge.
or
1B. From Hayes & Harlington railway station follow Station Approach to the A312 (Station Road), turning right. Very shortly afterwards you will cross the Grand Union Canal; turn right on to Western View. Take the canal path eastwards for about 1km (c½ mile) and turn left at Bull's Bridge.

2. Follow the canal path. There are strict restrictions on cycling in places on the path, particularly at the eastern end where there are houseboats: follow them assiduously. The canal enters the Maida Hill Tunnel just after Little Venice; dismount at Regent's Park Zoo as the canal is banned to cyclists. To rejoin the canal to continue to Limehouse Basin see Route 12.

Starting Points: Brentford Lock (1A) or Hayes & Harlington railway station (1B).

Parking: No specific car parks, but on-street parking is available in the area.

Public Transport: Trains to Hayes & Harlington (the station before West Drayton) run half-hourly from Paddington on the line to Slough.

Links to Other Paths: Links with the Grand Union Canal, Routes 9 and 10; links with Route 3 at Kew; links at the eastern end with Route 12.

Distance: c22km (c14 miles) from Bull's Bridge to Little Venice.

Map: Explorer 173.

Surfaces and Gradients: No gradients; the canal towpath varies from very good to good but can get a bit muddy if wet.

Roads and Crossings: Some roadwork required from stations and at the eastern

GRAND UNION CANAL —
THE REGENT'S ARM
(Camden Lock to Limehouse Basin)

Rejoining the canal after the hiatus caused by the tunnel and Regent's Park, from the lively buzz of Camden Lock Market this route wends its way through the railway lines and gasworks of King's Cross, through Islington to the substantial green space of Victoria Park. It's an oasis of calm amongst the rush — exemplified dramatically when you have to follow a road route while the canal is in the Islington Tunnel. Still, the road route does allow you to enjoy detours to Chapel Street fruit and vegetable market or to the antique shops of Camden Passage off Upper Street.

PLACES OF INTEREST

Camden Lock

The canal runs straight through the middle of Camden, with the Lock right beside the Market. Heading west, just after Camden Lock are the futuristic canal flats designed by Nicholas Grimshaw looking like an aluminium space station. Grimshaw also designed the Sainsbury supermarket close by the flats, a similarly sci-fi edifice.

Camden's main attraction is the large weekend market, which is mainly for tourists and the young and trendy, noteworthy primarily for the fashion bargains to be had for those who can handle the crowds. Shoes, leather goods and predominantly ethnic and youth tribal bohemian gear are to the fore but there are also stalls selling postwar and retro furniture, and lighting. Nearby, there's Jongleurs Comedy Store, the famous Jazz Café on Parkway, the French

Café down Delancey Street that has a stream of rich and famous dropped off and picked up at its entrance, and Compendium, renowned as the best alternative bookshop in London. It is also true that Camden is popular with students. Clubs — The Electric Ballroom, WKD's, The Underground, Camden Palace, The Laurel Tree and HQ's — are all known for hosting happening nights and have cashed in on the student contingent. Pubs such as The World's End (next to the tube; a regular meeting place), Liberty's (Irish pub on High Street) and The Good Mixer (formerly Blur's hangout; behind the market) complete the entertainment on offer. And with a couple of well-stocked bookshops, cheap market clothes, shoes and records, tucked-away cafes and cheap eats, the park, the canal and regular night bus services, it is no surprise that the students have moved in.

Limehouse Basin

Formerly known as Regent's Canal Dock, this is where the Grand Union Canal and the River Lea join the Thames. At one time this was the London entrance to the entire countrywide canal network and as such was controlled by the British Waterways Board. The entrance to the basin is at the apex of the Thames's curve on the north bank. The cut was opened in 1820 and later a dock for vessels known as Limehouse Basin was made. The dock provided 4ha (10 acres) of water and roughly 1.6ha (4 acres) of quays and wharves. After a general

Right: **The gasometers behind Kings Cross are a well-known North London landmark.**

decline in water trade with the building of Tilbury Docks down river, the Basin declined in use until it ceased operating in 1969. Only pleasure craft go to and fro here now. The area as a whole is being extensively renovated with many of the old warehouses being turned into sought-after luxury flats.

Canary Wharf

Brave or misguided? Only history will be able to judge fully the decision to regenerate London's docklands: what can be said today is that the spectacular architecture of the centrepiece,

particularly the 243.8m (800ft)-high 50-storey tower, has given East London an aura of modernity that will take many years to wear off. Helped by architects of the calibre of Pei, Cobb, Freed & Partners and Cesar Pelli & Associates (who designed the tower), masterplanners Skidmore, Owings & Merrill turned an area that was under-utilised into a thriving commercial centre. The development of the Thames side from Tower Bridge to Greenwich and the Isle of Dogs, much of it involving the refurbishment of splendid old buildings, makes a fantastic cycling day out with almost too much to take in!

Starting Points: By road from Little Venice and Route 11 (1A); by train from Camden Town station (1B).

Parking: Street parking all around Camden but it can be very busy even on Sunday mornings.

Public Transport: Camden station is on the North London Line (three trains an hour from Richmond to North Woolwich).

Links to Other Paths: Route 11 in the west; Route 13 in the east.

Distance: 14.5km (9 miles) from Little Venice to Limehouse Basin.

Map: Explorer 173.

Surfaces and Gradients: The canal towpath is uniformly excellent; there are no gradients of any note.

Roads and Crossings: The Islington Tunnel requires about a mile of road cycling. Otherwise there are busy roads in Camden to get on to the canal and varying amounts of road use at the other end depending on your choice of route.

Refreshments: Camden Lock, Islington and canalside pubs.

Route Instructions: 1A. Take Blomfield Road to the Edgware Road.
or

1B. From Camden Road railway station, see below.

2. Turn left and then right on to St John's Wood Road.

3. At the roundabout turn on to the A41 (Park Road) turning left after the Mosque on to Hanover Gardens that will take you into Regent's Park.

4. Turn left and follow the Outer Circle around to exit through Gloucester Gardens.

5. Turn left on to the A4201 (Albany Street, and then continue straight on to Parkway. At Camden High Street (Camden Town underground) turn left and follow the instructions below (1B).
or
1B. From Camden Road railway station proceed to Camden Lock by turning left on Bonny Street and then right on to Camden Road. Follow Camden Road down to Camden Underground station past the top of Kentish Town Road. Loop round to the other entrance of the Underground on Camden High Street.

6. Turn right and follow the road down till it becomes Chalk Farm Road and goes over the canal with a humped bridge.

7. Turn left immediately after the bridge and go down to Camden Lock and the canal towpath.

8. Cycle down to the second lock with the

Breakfast TV studios on the opposite side, their giant eggcups on the skyline.

9. After a mile or two, the gasometers of King's Cross appear, then King's Cross Lock and moorings.

10. 1.6km (1 mile) beyond this marks the beginning of the Islington Tunnel. Possessing no towpath, the tunnel necessitates a brief street diversion.

11. Ascend on to Muriel Street and follow into Rodney Street in a southerly direction.

12. Rodney Street leads into Pentonville Road, where you turn left and proceed up the hill.

13. On reaching the Angel, cross over the top of Upper Street and walk past the Angel Underground station down City Road. (At Upper Street you can divert to Camden Passage antique shops by turning left to go up the east side of Upper Street. The antiques start a couple of hundred metres up on your right around Duncan Street.)

14. Walking down City Road on its left-hand side, take the third turning on the left: Colebrook Row.

15. Walk down Colebrook Row till you cross over the canal and rejoin the towpath by turning immediately right into Noel Road, where the entrance is situated.

16. The canal runs along the outside of Victoria Park. You can now join Route 13 or simply continue to Limehouse Basin.

17. Exit the canal on to the A13 (Commercial Road) before reaching the basin, and make your way to Limehouse railway station or continue on to join the Thames riverside path.

Below: Canal sides make safe cycle tracks for children.

Left: The cranes will not leave Canary Wharf for some years, but Pelli's Tower stands above it all for the moment.

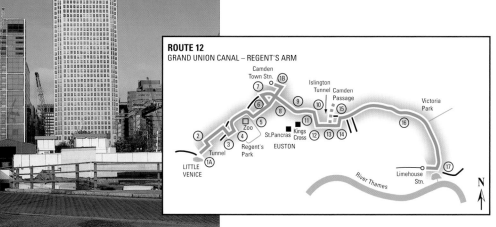

ROUTE 12
GRAND UNION CANAL – REGENT'S ARM

ROUTE 13

HACKNEY WICK– LIMEHOUSE LOOP

This route covers a pleasant circle from Hackney Wick station, through Victoria Park, along the Regent's Canal, Limehouse Cut and back along the lower part of the River Lea. Anyone unused to East London will be surprised by the area: today Limehouse, on the fringe of the Canary Wharf and Isle of Dogs regeneration area, contrasts strongly with the quiet greenery of Victoria Park and the Lea & Stort Navigation.

PLACES OF INTEREST

Victoria Park

Following devastating outbreaks of cholera and typhoid as well as general pestilence and poor living conditions in the East End, a petition of 30,000 signatures was collected by two local MPs and presented to Queen Victoria in 1839. They were demanding a new park to provide an open space for public recreation. Two years later the government agreed to provide Victoria Park as the first large-scale, non-profit-making public amenity provided free at state expense for the use of the lower orders. Consequently, an area of some 87.8ha (217 acres) of deserted gravel pits and desultory market gardens was acquired and the official government architect, James Pennethorne, appointed to plan the park out. It is 2km (1.25 miles) long and 0.8km (½-mile) wide. The lakes were dug in 1846, when plenty of trees were planted.

Right: An entrance to Victoria Park.

In the late 19th century 10,000 people would come to wash in the lake between 6 and 8 o'clock each morning, and in the summer heatwaves up to 25,000 people would squeeze in. On Sundays big crowds would arrive to listen to religious and political rallies. During World War 2 anti-aircraft batteries were stationed in the park but in common with much of the East End it received heavy bomb damage.

In 1988 a comprehensive restoration of the park was begun to revive its former Victorian glory. In the southeast corner are two of the recesses from the old London Bridge which was demolished in 1832. The park remains a popular recreational area with locals.

Docklands Light Railway

The DLR (Docklands Light Railway) is a computer-operated overhead railway linking the City of London to Docklands at Stratford, Beckton and Island Gardens. It is fully automated and driverless, although there is a member of staff on every train. The DLR crosses the Isle of Dogs and runs almost as far as the Tower of London to Bank and Tower Gateway. A new extension called the Lewisham Link has been added to the existing DLR network and is a joint government/private sector project. The DLR runs every day of the year except Christmas Day: every 4-8 minutes at peak times; every 8-12 minutes off-peak and weekends and every 12 minutes early morning and late at night. Scandalously, only collapsible bicycles are allowed on it.

Left: East-Enders used to come every day to bathe in Victoria Park.

the Lea & Stort; and following Route 6 down the Isle of Dogs links up with Greenwich and Routes 7, 8 and 27.

Distance: c10km (6¼ miles).

Map: Explorer 162 and 173.

Surfaces and Gradients: No gradients of note; the path can be difficult in places when wet.

Roads and Crossings: Little road use unless necessitated by conditions. Grove Road in Victoria Park needs care.

Refreshments: A variety of pubs and amenities, including excellent bagels from the VIP Bagel Shop on Gore Road, and a number of pubs around Victoria Park.

Starting Points: Victoria Park car park (1A) or Hackney Wick railway station (1B).

Parking: Car park in Victoria Park. Street parking all around the area.

Public Transport: Rail services to Hackney Wick on the North London Line from Richmond to North Woolwich.

Links to Other Paths: Links directly to Routes 6, 12 and 15; Route 14 is further up

Above: River Lea on a sunny day.

Route Instructions:

1B. From the station take Wallis Road, crossing the A115 (Chapman Road) and the A102M by the footbridge.

2. Entering Victoria Park, turn right and cycle around the park, crossing Grove Road by the car park (1A).

3. Join the canal whenever you want.

4. Continue to Limehouse Basin.

5. Join the Limehouse Cut and follow the canal to the junction with the River Lea.

6. Follow the Lea Navigation until the A115 (Whitepost Lane).

7. Follow the lane as it turns right to Hackney Wick station.

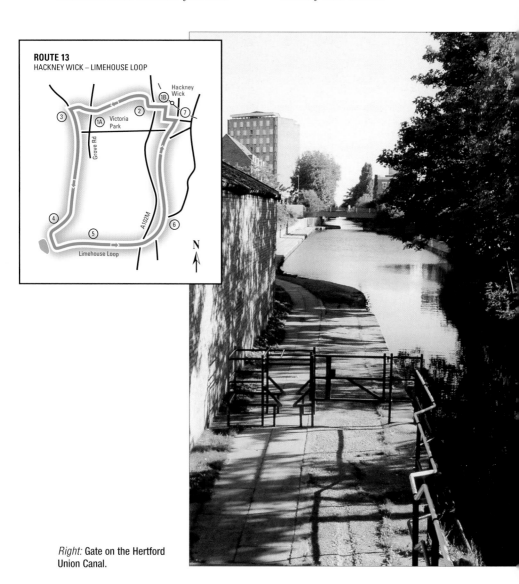

ROUTE 13
HACKNEY WICK – LIMEHOUSE LOOP

Right: **Gate on the Hertford Union Canal.**

WALTON'S WALK

This is a gentle, short cycle ride that is perfect for a young family. It can easily be extended to Broxbourne further up the Lea or southward as far as one cares to cycle. OS Explorer 174 identifies the permutations clearly. Walton Lock Bridge affords an intimate view of the workings of the lock below.

Izaak Walton (1593–1683)

Best known for *The Compleat Angler*, or the *Contemplative Man's Recreation* (1653), Walton was born in the parish of St Mary, Staffordshire. He started his working life as an ironmonger, and in 1618 became a freeman of the Ironmongers' Company and made his fortune. While living in London he would often fish in the Tottenham area, which is why Walton's Walk is so named. A friend of two of the century's most important poets, John Donne and fishing companion George Herbert, Walton's modest beginnings did not prevent him from becoming a significant and learned biographer — as well as Donne (1640) and Herbert (1670), he also wrote biographies of theologians Hooker (1665) and Sanderson, Bishop of Lincoln (1678). Walton left London during the Civil War and ended his years living at Farnham Castle as the permanent guest of George Morley, Bishop of Winchester. He died in

Winchester on 15 December 1683. *The Compleat Angler* is one of the most reprinted books in the English language; one of the reasons is that it is more than a treatise. It is more literary than scientific, focusing on three hunters — a fisherman (Piscator, who is Walton himself), a huntsman (Venator) and a fowler (Auceps) — who travel along the River Lea discussing their pastimes.

Walton's Walk Mosaics

Two commemorative mosaics by Norma Vondee have been placed by the Environment Agency on large standing stones at the beginning and end of the walk to mark the improvement and completion of the pathway. The southern mosaic represents the dawn and the northern mosaic dusk. The southern mosaic features a sunrise and the work is angled to face southeast to catch the early morning sun. An alternative interpretation is that it shows an explosion with swirls of smoke — this is a reference to the Royal Gunpowder factory which used to be sited nearby. The factory made gunpowder since the 17th century, and local rumour insists that Guy Fawkes used some of the explosives in his attempt to blow up Parliament in 1605.

Left: Family cycling along the River Lea.

Above: Another scene along the River Lea.

Starting Points: Walton's Walk car park (1A), Waltham Cross railway station (1B) or Theobald's Grove station (1C).

Parking: Walton's Walk car park, plus many other car parks, for example at Cheshunt Junction, River Lea Country Park, etc.

Public Transport: Trains to Waltham Cross run half-hourly from Liverpool Street on the Cambridge line.

Links to Other Paths: Route 12 can be extended by continuing up the Lea River towpath to Waltham Lock.

Distance: 5km (3 miles) easily doubled by extending up to Broxbourne.

Map: Explorer 174.

Surfaces and Gradients: No gradients; good surfaces for cycling.

Roads and Crossings: Road from the two stations, otherwise off-road.

Refreshments: Pubs at Waltham Lock and in Waltham Abbey.

Route Instructions: 1A. Leave the car park at Waltham Lock, also called Walton's Walk car park. Cross Waltham Lock and bear right along the bank of Horsemill Stream, the old overflow channel of the Lea.
or
1B. From Waltham Cross railway station turn right on to the A121 (Eleanor Cross Road/Station Road) and turn left just before Waltham Lock to the signposted car park.
or
1C. From Theobald's Grove station follow Trinity Lane to Marsh Bridge following the path to the right to reach the starting point of this route.

2. Here one reaches a possible permutation, for a route goes off across Waltham Marsh to the left. It can be connected once again to this route at Powdermill Cut (if you go right).

3. At the weir there is another possible left turn — the nearer end of Powdermill Cut.

4. Continuing on you reach the furthest limit of Walton's Walk at Hook Marsh. There is also a car park here. You can

continue cycling north at this point if you wish, crossing the river by a footbridge and rejoining the towpath just past the electricity substation. You can also substantially extend the route by cycling to Broxbourne and back: the path is described in detail on the OS Explorer 174.

5. Turning left one follows the path alongside Turnershill Marsh. (Here you can also turn right to loop up to Nazeing Marsh or go straight on. The latter direction takes you to the railway line and a left turn then takes you back to Cheshunt station and, further on, Marsh Bridge.) Further on our route another left turn is required on to the path running between Cheshunt Lake and Turnershill Marsh.

6. Turn right here to get back to Marsh Bridge and left to go back to the car park and lock.

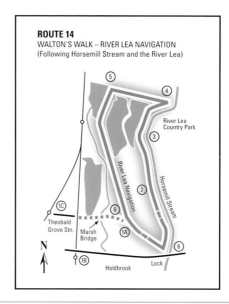

ROUTE 14
WALTON'S WALK – RIVER LEA NAVIGATION
(Following Horsemill Stream and the River Lea)

Above: Friend's Bridge over the River Lea.

THE LEA & STORT FROM HACKNEY WICK TO ENFIELD LOCK

The Lea (or Lee, both spellings are used) & Stort Navigation from Limehouse up to Bishop's Stortford (c55km [34 miles] up the River Stort) or Hertford (44km [27½ miles] up the River Lea) makes an excellent day's cycle for those wishing to go some distance. This section of the navigation looks at a shorter 15km (9-mile) stretch.

PLACES OF INTEREST

Hackney Marshes

The marshes are the flood plain of the River Lea and were originally crossed by a causeway built by the Romans. They comprise around 136ha (337 acres) of meadowland, open grassland, scrub and large trees to the east of Hackney. The area was bought by London County Council in 1893 for £75,000. The Marshes regularly flooded until the canals were dug in the 19th century. A wide variety of birds, plants and animals live on the Marshes which have now become synonymous with football as hundreds of pitches are now laid out there. Hackney Marshes make up part of the Lea Valley Regional Park, a huge green corridor linking parks, reservoirs, marshlands, meadows, filter beds, football and cricket pitches and waterways between Ware in Hertfordshire and the Thames. The area is designed to provide a huge range of recreational facilities with everything from cycling, cricket, football, canoeing, pony trekking, walking and sailing for northeast Londoners.

Lea Valley Park

The Lea Valley Regional Park Authority was established in 1967 to regenerate what was a derelict sprawl of industrial units. It performed its job brilliantly and the Lea Valley today is a green corridor with restoration and regeneration having a profound impact on the quality of the environment with a unique mix of farmland, nature reserves, open green spaces and waterways, inlaid with sports and leisure, heritage and entertainment centres. Sites include Walthamstow Marsh, a Site of Special Scientific Interest that has never been developed; Cornmill Meadows, the best site for dragonflies in Essex, Herts and Greater London; Walthamstow Reservoirs, where birds overwinter — ducks, geese and heron colonies; Waltham Abbey Woods, a wildlife refuge closed to public access; Middlesex Filter Beds, a derelict filtration plant reclaimed as a nature reserve; Rye Meads SSSI with its kingfishers and common terns; and much, much more. The excellent leaflets on the Lea Valley Park and other publications can be acquired from Lea Valley Park Information Centre, Abbey Gardens, Waltham Abbey, Essex EN9 1XQ.

Starting Point: Hackney Wick railway station (1A) or B112 car park (1B).

Parking: Off B112 (Homerton Road) or A104 (Lee Bridge Road).

Public Transport: Rail services to Hackney Wick railway station are provided three trains an hour by the North London Line from Richmond to North Woolwich.

Links to Other Paths: Links to Routes 9, 10, 11 and 25.

Distance: 15km (9 miles); 30km (18¾ miles) round trip.

Map: Explorer 174.

Surfaces and Gradients: No gradients; good paths.

Roads and Crossings: Road from the stations only.

Refreshments: Many pubs just off the route — at Lea Bridge, in Clapton; Ponders End and Enfield Lock (the Greyhound). Café next to the Rowing Club at (9).

Route Instructions: 1A. Leave Hackney Wick railway station, turning left on to Wallis Road, and then take the first left into White Post Lane. This leads into Carpenters Road on the right-hand side of which you can descend to the towpath of the Lea Navigation. Head northwards.

Above: There are many access points to north-east London from the River Lea: this is at Clapton.

or

1B. Leave the car park and turn right on to Homerton Road. Join the towpath before the bridge.

2. Go under the Eastway flyover and past Hackney Marshes football fields.

3. Just before the Navigation ends and rejoins the Lea are the Middlesex Filter Beds, now a charming nature reserve.

4. Crossing over the river the route leads past a pub and under Lea Bridge Road. (Join here if you parked at the A104 car parks.)

5. Further on, a bridge over the river allows travel on either side. The further bank gives on to various nature reserves, an ancient lammas ground, walks and parks and other amenities, including Lea Valley Equestrian Centre and the ice rink.

6. Further still another bridge allows further options of travel on either side.

Left: Narrow boats on the Lea.

Above: There are many sites of Victorian industrial archaeology along the river.

7. At the end of Walthamstow Marsh Nature Reserve and Park the reservoirs prevent further waterside travel.

8. Another (metalled) bridge allows you to cross by Springfield Marina.

9. Go over to the corner of Springfield Park. Now turn to the right. Continue on this side, towards Tottenham.

10. Passing Markfield Park with its Beam Engine Museum, one reaches . . .

11. . . .Tottenham Hale and Tottenham Lock. The towpath remains on this side.

12. At Stonebridge Lock the route crosses the water again. Continue northwards . . .

13. . . . past Picketts Lock . . .

14. . . . past Ponders End Lock, Brimsdown and the Swan and Pike Pool . . .

15. . . . to Enfield Lock, where the Lea and the Lea Navigation run side by side. Once again the route swaps sides.

16. At the lock you can take the path to

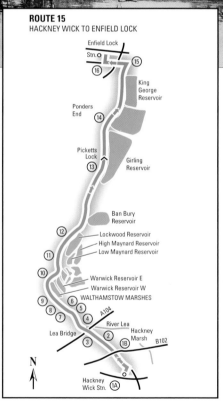

ROUTE 15
HACKNEY WICK TO ENFIELD LOCK

Enfield Lock railway station or retrace your steps. Get to the railway by means of the Prince of Wales footpath, crossing the A1055 and railway by means of a footbridge and turning right on Bradley Road.

Left: There are a couple of surprisingly steep slopes in Richmond Park: if you aren't confident get off and walk.

trees by the deer cropping the branches to a level height. The main gates are at Richmond, Ham, Kingston, Kingston Hill (Robin Hood roundabout), Roehampton and Sheen. Two huge lakes called Pen Ponds are magnets for waterfowl and a popular dog-walking spot.

Around London
RICHMOND PARK

This is the largest open space in urban Britain and unlike all the other royal parks it is still kept relatively wild and unkempt as a deer park, although tarmac roads and solid paths criss-cross the park. It was established as a royal park by Charles I in 1637 (to replace Hyde Park which he had just opened to the public) who surrounded its 999.5ha (2,470 acres) with a high wall. Locals were allowed limited access to collect firewood. Eventually, a judge ordered that ladders could be erected wherever the wall crossed a public right of way. Now the public has free access by motorcar between dawn and dusk, leaving the 700-odd red and fallow deer at peace. The park is a large area of grass and woodlands and in the summer bracken covers much of the ground; it is used by walkers, riders and cyclists who come from miles around to enjoy the fresh air. Apart from the occasional but stunning views of London, in the middle of the park you can imagine yourself deep in the English countryside despite the appearance of neatness given to the

PLACES OF INTEREST

Isabella Plantation
This woodland garden is at its best from mid-April until the end of May when the hundreds of rhododendrons (many of them rare), camellias and azaleas are in flower and the spring bulbs are out. The plantation dates from 1823 and is fenced in to prevent the park's deer from ravaging the trees and plants.

White Lodge
This one-time royal residence on Spanker's Hill has been the country home of the Royal Ballet School since 1955. A Palladian villa commissioned by George II and built in 1727, the original house has been considerably extended. The future Edward VIII was born here in 1894 and the Duke and Duchess of York (later King George VI and Queen Elizabeth) lived here for a few years after their marriage.

Star and Garter Home
This home for wounded servicemen is built on the site of the famously fashionable Star and Garter Inn which had its heyday in the 18th and early 19th century when the fresh country airs of Richmond Hill were a popular meeting place for London society.

It was patronised by many famous people including Charles Dickens and Louis-Philippe, who stayed here for six months after fleeing from Paris, and Napoleon III even had apartments here. The original inn was rebuilt by new owners in the 1860s as a French Renaissance château to considerable public ridicule. But by the end of the century after a couple of disastrous fires the building was left empty.

During World War 1 it was used as a temporary hospital for troops and in 1916 became a home for disabled soldiers. Its use was now established but after such a devastating conflict the accommodation was insufficient and the building was pulled down and replaced by a new red brick building designed by Sir Edwin Cooper and completed in 1924.

Starting Points: Car park at Pembroke Lodge (1A), Norbiton station (1B) close to Kingston Gate and Richmond station (1C) close to Richmond Gate.

Parking: There are a number of car parks in Richmond Park at Pembroke Lodge (1A), Kingston Gate, Robin Hood Gate, Pen Ponds, Roehampton Gate (bike hire available from this one in the summer), and East Sheen Gate.

Public Transport: See Routes 2 and 3.

Links to Other Paths: Links to Routes 2, 3, and 4.

Distance: c11km (7 miles).

Map: Explorer 161.

Surfaces and Gradients: Excellent shared path with pedestrians (so cycle carefully). Two short hills which can be avoided if you're unfit or just chicken.

Roads and Crossings: Road to the park from each station; the path also crosses roads at each of the gates. These roads can be busy (although there are no commercial vehicles in the park) so take care in crossing them.

Refreshments: Pembroke Lodge offers a sit-down tea room; there are sales facilities in each of the car parks, and pubs galore close to all the gates in Richmond, Ham, Sheen and Kingston.

Route Instructions: 1A. Turn left or right

Below: The metalled road from Pen Ponds car park to Ham Gate is a useful shortcut towards Wimbledon.

Left: Pen Ponds make an ideal spot for a picnic.

left goes first to Sheen and then on towards Roehampton.

or

1C. From Norbiton station turn right and immediately left down Wolverton Avenue. At the T-junction with the A308 (Kingston Hill) cross the road carefully, turning right and immediately left to go down Queens Road leading to Kingston Gate.

4. Taking the left-hand path will lead to Pembroke Lodge and Richmond; the right will circle the park with the first gate (5) being that off the A3 at Robin Hood roundabout (where there is a link via a footbridge to Route 17).

6. At Robin Hood Gate roundabout you can take the road to Pen Ponds, branching left (7) along a metalled road to Ham Gate (through which one can get to Ham House on Route 2) or continuing past the White Lodge (8) to the Sheen Gate roundabout.

Note: most other paths in Richmond Park are banned for cyclists — particularly the good-looking off-road terrain. The use of paths in Richmond Park has been a contentious issue, so stay legal!

to start the circuit of the park. It's well-signposted and not difficult to follow.

or

1B. From Richmond station turn left on to the one-way system, following it round Eton Street, Paradise Road and Red Lion Street, turning left to go up Hill Street. Go over the roundabout at the head of Richmond Bridge, taking the left fork to go up Richmond Hill.

or

1C. From Norbiton station, see below.

2. Pause to enjoy the 'matchless view of the River Thames' from the top and continue past the Star and Garter Home . . .

3. . . . . entering the park at Richmond Gate. Take the right-hand path that leads towards Pembroke Lodge and Kingston Gate; the

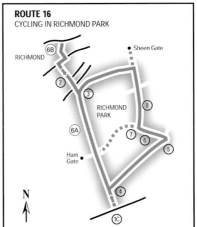

ROUTE 16
CYCLING IN RICHMOND PARK

Left: Shared paths are always thronged with pedestrians on fine days: dismount and walk your bike as necessary.

WIMBLEDON COMMON AND PUTNEY HEATH

Comprising 445ha (1,100 acres) of unenclosed land, Wimbledon Common is a popular location for walking and cycling. Throughout the 19th century the common was used to review Army Volunteers, and the National Rifle Association held its competitions here between 1860 and 1890 before moving to Bisley. On the west side of the common lies Cannizaro House, a Georgian mansion which has now become local government offices but the fine gardens containing rare trees, follies and an Italian garden are open to the public. On Windmill Road lies the only 'hollow post' mill in the country.

PLACES OF INTEREST

Caesar's Camp

Probably a Stone Age earthwork which had absolutely nothing to do with any Romans, let alone Caesar. Until 1875 it had huge circular earthworks with steep ramparts and deep ditches, but the Lord of the Manor wanted to build on the site and started flattening it out until stopped by a High Court order — unfortunately too late as the damage was already done.

All England Lawn Tennis and Croquet Club

The home of English tennis and the setting for the Wimbledon Championships every June, one of the four major Grand Slam tournaments and the only one still played on grass courts. The club has been here since 1922 when it moved from Worple Road. It is a private tennis club for which there is a waiting list. The Lawn Tennis Association (founded 1888), the governing body of the game in Britain, runs the championship jointly with the club. Recently modernised to provide the latest facilities and increased capacity, the club has two covered courts and 16 outside grass courts.

Left: The windmill on Wimbledon Common. Inside there's a museum explaining the history and development of windmills, as well as working models, tools and machinery.

Starting Points: Robin Hood Roundabout (1A), Windmill Road car park (1B), Wimbledon railway station (1C).

Parking: Around the common there's a lot of parking, particularly along Cannizaro Road, Westside and Southside Common. There's a car park in the middle next to the Windmill Museum.

Public Transport: Regular trains to Wimbledon from Waterloo.

Links to Other Paths: Links directly with Route 16 and by road with Route 4.

Distance: From Robin Hood Roundabout (1A) to (3) c2km (1¼ miles); from (3) to (7) c5.5km (3½ miles).

Map: Explorer 161.

Surfaces and Gradients: Good, if occasionally muddy, earth and gravel bridlepaths. Short gradients with little severity.

Roads and Crossings: The A3 at Robin Hood Roundabout is extremely busy as can be Wimbledon Park Side, Putney Hill, and Roehampton Lane. Putney Heath Road is quieter. The route from the station isn't long (just over a kilometre [c¾ mile]), but the hill will prove quite steep for young legs and Wimbledon Hill Road is a busy thoroughfare.

Refreshments: Many good pubs and restaurants in Wimbledon Village; the Green Man on Putney Heath is to be recommended as are the Friend in Hand and Crooked Billet off Woodhayes Road. There is a café at the Windmill car park.

Route Instructions: 1A. From Robin Hood Roundabout head towards London, entering the common by the playing fields.
or
1B. From the Windmill car park, see below.
or
1C. From Wimbledon station turn right, pushing the bike to the bottom of Wimbledon Hill Road. Cycle up the hill going straight over on to the High Street at the top. Turn left along The Causeway and then on to Camp Road to reach (3).

2. This path leads up towards the Coombe Lane intersection with the A3, but it's best to turn left as signposted (there are clearly

marked cycle and bridlepaths on the common).

3. Here you can go right to look at Caesar's Camp, straight on to end up at the Crooked Billet and Hand in Hand (9) or Wimbledon station (1C), or left towards the Windmill Museum and golf club.

4. Continue past Windmill Road car park (1B) towards Tibbet's Corner.

5. Take the subway on to Putney Heath and continue alongside the A219 (Tibbet's Ride) . . .

6. . . . until you reach the bus park (and refreshment kiosk) at the bottom. The Green Man is opposite here on Putney Heath.

7. Turn left at Medfield Street and then join the horse ride as the road turns sharply downhill.

8. Take the subway under the A3 and rejoin the circuit at the Windmill.

ROUTE 17
WIMBLEDON COMMON

Below: **The path leading from Putney Heath to the subway back to Wimbledon Common.**

RIVER CRANE

(from Twickenham to the A315 and back)

This is a short, there-and-back trip through Crane Park, an island of wildlife along the River Crane, and a tribute to such organisations as the London Wildlife Trust that do so much to protect urban wildlife. It's short and gentle and takes you close to two major sporting locations: The Stoop, the home of Harlequins Rugby Football Club, and the head-quarters of the game of rugby, Twickenham itself.

PLACES OF INTEREST

Powder Mills, Crane Park

Gunpowder has been a traditional local industry along the River Crane since at least the mid-16th century. One of the first mills was near Baber Bridge, while the last mills to close were the Hounslow Powder Mills, which stopped grinding in 1920. These gunpowder mills were notorious for their frequent explosions; Horace Walpole complained of one in particular in January 1772 which damaged his new house at Strawberry Hill. There still remain some remnants of the manufacture of gunpowder in Crane Park in the shape of the wheel pits and machine bases, as well as the high earth mounds which were built up around the small grinding sheds to shield the blast if an explosion should occur. Interestingly, there is also a shot tower — a conical brick tower around 24m (80ft) high that used to have a shallow conical lead roof surrounded by a timber bellcote. The tower is dated 1828, although the inscription saying so above the doorway has long vanished. Sadly, this tower is unlikely to have been used for casting lead shot — it is more likely to have been a water tower for firefighting purposes or for the use of hydraulic equipment.

London Wildlife Trust

In its own words, 'The London Wildlife

Dead and alive!

Above: The London Wildlife Trust is a major force for good, fighting to sustain and enhance London's wildlife habitats. Join it.

Trust fights to sustain and enhance London's wildlife habitats to create a city richer in wildlife'. To this end the Trust encourages interest in and knowledge of the huge variety of wildlife issues particularly relevant to Londoners, and encourages them to become actively involved in matters which have a bearing on the natural environment. Through lectures, outdoor activities and publications the Trust informs Londoners about their city and provides an influential voice across the boroughs whose political decisions may impact on animals, plants and the environment in general.

Twickenham Rugby Ground

The home of the English Rugby Football Union and known affectionately as 'Headquarters', it has been rebuilt over the last 20 years to become a massive national stadium. The original site of 4ha (10.25 acres) was bought in 1907 for £5,572 12s 6d by William Williams and the ground soon had a capacity of 30,000 spectators. In 1921

a further 2.8ha (7 acres) were bought and since then the ground has been continually improved and the capacity increased. In 1981 a new south stand was built to accommodate 12,854; but this has now been dwarfed by the newer stands. Nevertheless, getting a ticket for the Six Nations Tournament (until 1999 the Five Nations) is near-impossible without influence in the right places.

Above: The River Crane reaches the River Thames near the Richmond Tidal Barrage. It is very well sign-posted although starts as a walk.

Starting Points: Twickenham railway station (1A) and car park next to the station in Twickenham (1B).

Parking: Multi-storey near the station; meter and other car parks all over the area.

Public Transport: Regular trains out of Waterloo.

Links to Other Paths: Route 2.

Distance: A c8km (5-mile) round trip from Twickenham station. This route can be linked to Richmond via the A316, along most of which is a shared pedestrian/cyclepath.

Map: Explorer 161.

Surfaces and Gradients: Good metalled paths and roads.

Roads and Crossings: The London Road in Twickenham is very busy.

Refreshments: Good pubs in Twickenham, particularly down by the river.

Route Instructions: 1A. Turn left out of Twickenham railway station on to the London Road.
or
1B. Come out of the car park next to the station in Twickenham (1A) and turn left on to Arragon Road.

Left: The route becomes a shared pedestrian and cycle path in Twickenham.

2. Cross the road on to Railway Approach and turn right and then left into Station Road.

3. Continue along Lion Road.

4. Turn right into Edwin Road and go under the railway bridge, turning right on to Marsh Farm Road.

5. Cross the railway by the footbridge.

6. Pass by the Stoop, taking the path under the railway bridge.

7. Cross the Crane and then, almost immediately, recross into the park.

8. Continue up the park, passing the under the A316 (9) and by the Shot Tower (10).

11. Either join the A315, retrace your steps to Twickenham or go back to the A316 and follow the shared pedestrian/ cycle path which will take you to Sunbury or Richmond.

ROUTE 18
RIVER CRANE

Above: Path alongside the railway with Twickenham rugby ground in the background.

RIVER WANDLE
(from Mitcham to Wimbledon)

The Wandle rises at Croydon, is fed by springs at Carshalton and joined by the River Graveney at Tooting, and enters the Thames at Wandsworth which takes its name from the river. It drops at an average rate of 14ft per mile over its 11-mile course. This rapid course accounts for why this tributary of the Thames has been used for centuries for its water power — the Domesday Book registers 13 corn mills on the Wandle. At one time there were over 100 mills within a 14.4km (9-mile) stretch of the river and in the early 18th century it drove 68 waterwheels. In 1880 there were more than 30 mills between Croydon and Wandsworth working a huge variety of materials — for copper, oil, leather, tobacco, snuff, flour, paper and parchment.

At one time Admiral Nelson fished in the Wandle from the bottom of Lady Hamilton's garden at Merton Place; she even diverted part of it to form an ornamental water garden which she christened the 'Nile' in his honour. Now, thanks in part to the River Wandle Open Spaces Society which started work before the war, the river leads a peaceful existence with herons and kingfishers living beside the waters which are a haven for insects and fish of many kinds, including the now rare freshwater shrimp.

PLACES OF INTEREST

Mitcham Common
These 186ha (460 acres) of Surrey common ground were formalised under an Act of 1891 to provide for the running of the land by a Board of Conservators. Famously dangerous for highwaymen and assorted miscreants in the past, as with other similar areas, the common was particularly renowned for its summer horse sales; these have now stopped to be replaced (in part) by an annual summer fair on 12–14 August on the Three Kings Piece. In 1848 the Chartists used the common as their assembly point before marching to protest their grievances to Parliament. During World War 2 anti-aircraft batteries were installed here to defend London. Today the common is criss-crossed by roads and railways and includes a golf course, sports grounds and a sewage farm.

Morden Hall Park
Now a deer park, in the early 19th century weatherboarded snuff mills worked here, powered by waterwheels. The last working mill closed in 1922. The park itself was left to the National Trust on the death of Gilliat Hatfield, a local wealthy philanthropist whose family had made their fortune from snuff milling. Some 19th-century grinding stones can be seen outside the Century Mill. To make snuff, tobacco leaves were dried in kilns next to the mill. When

Right: The Wandle Industrial Museum produces an excellent and informative map of the Wandle Trail. Morden Hall Park is owned by the National Trust and has an excellent garden centre.

brittle enough, the leaves were ground into powder. The park contains another Georgian mansion built in 1770 for John Ewart, a London distiller and merchant who enclosed the park. The building is now used by the Parks Department of the local council.

Liberty Board Mill

Best known as Merton Mills, Liberty Board Mill is a craft centre and museum and a listed building. French Huguenots settled here to escape religious oppression at home, bringing with them their silk industry, calico bleaching and printing skills — all using the particularly good water of the Wandle. As a legacy of their endeavour, the Arts and Crafts instigator, William Morris, brought his workshop here in 1881 (unfortunately it was destroyed in the 1940s) and the Regent Street store Liberty also had its print works here.

Starting Points: Mitcham Junction station (1) or start at Merton Mills (7) and cycle the other way.

Parking: Big car parks at the Savacentre in Merton and at Merton Mills. Car park at Morden Hall Park.

Public Transport: Regular train services to Mitcham Junction from Victoria and London Bridge, and via Thameslink.

Links to Other Paths: No direct links.

Distance: c1km (c½ mile) from Mitcham Junction station to (3); c7km (4½ miles) from (3) to Plough Lane football ground; c2km (1¼ miles) to Wimbledon station.

Map: Explorer 161.

Surfaces and Gradients: Good riverside path, mostly made up but with muddy and more difficult parts.

Roads and Crossings: Many; all should be treated carefully.

Refreshments: Many pubs and cafés en route — those at Merton Mills market and the tea rooms at Morden Hall Park are to be recommended.

Route Instructions:
Note: most of the parks and open spaces on

Above: Water wheel at Morden Hall Park.

Above: River Wandle at Morden Hall Park.

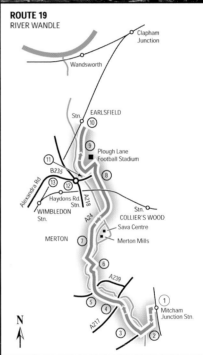

ROUTE 19
RIVER WANDLE

this route have interesting places to explore. The main route is a guide only — the well-situated maps provide on-the-spot information on locations and wildlife.

1. From the station turn left on to the A237 (Carshalton Road).

2. Turn right on to Goat Road.

3. Turn right on to Watermead Lane.

4. Continue past the National Trust watermeads and cross the busy A217 Bishopsford Road, turning right, joining the path on your left in Ravensbury Park.

5. Turn right on to the A239 (Morden Road) and then left into Morden Hall Park.

6. Meander through this splendid National Trust property, alongside which the new Croydon tram link will run.

7. The path continues past Merton Mills, under the A24 and past the Savacentre.

8. Then it's on towards the late, lamented Plough Lane, scene of so many of Wimbledon Association Football Club's triumphs.

9. If you wish to continue towards Earlsfield station, cross Plough Lane and continue along the river to Summerley Street, turning left (10) on to the A227 (Garratt Lane) and the station.

11. Alternatively you can take the B235 (Plough Lane), crossing over the roundabout (12).

13. Turn left onto Alexandra Road that takes you up to Wimbledon station.

ROUTE 20

NONSUCH PARK

This is a gentle area for a short cycle ride or to which one can take a young family. There is much to see but no real route as such. Just park and explore the area. The now-destroyed hunting palace of Nonsuch was built in 1538 by Henry VIII on the site of Merton Priory — one of the many foundations to be dissolved and appropriated by the Crown. To add insult to injury, the stones from the priory were used in the building of the palace that Henry intended to rival Cardinal Wolsey's Hampton Court. The palace was designed to be beyond compare — 'nonesuch' — and by all accounts went a long way to be so with the help of Italian craftsmen. The palace was not to his daughter Queen Mary's taste and she swapped it with the Earl of Arundel for estates in Suffolk. However, his other daughter, Elizabeth I, must have liked it as she lived much of her later life here. The palace was passed around, in and out of royal hands, until it became the possession of Lord Berkeley in 1682. He ended its story by demolishing the place. Archaeologists dug the site in 1959–60 when the foundations were revealed and mapped and many bits and pieces were found.

Stane Street

The A24 road that forms the northern boundary of Nonsuch Park is the old Roman road known as Stane Street which was built in AD43–4 to connect Londinium to Noviomagus (London to Chichester). The road follows the route taken by the Roman legate Vespasian (later emperor) and his II Legion, Augusta, in AD43 when he was setting out to subdue the southwest. In Roman times Noviomagus was the tribal capital of Sussex and an important port as well as a commercial and administrative centre. Originally Stane Street was 92km (57 miles) long and built in only four straight pieces known as alignments. It diverts for the first time near Ewell to follow the chalk formation, then later avoids Leith Hill and the steepest bits of the South Downs. The Romans built their roads to last: they were constructed on a wide raised causeway (agger) about 1.5m (5ft) high and around 7.3m (24ft) wide, made of a rammed mixture of local hard stone and shales topped with a layer of fine stone chippings. On either side of the road was a ditch and every 19km (12 miles) they built an inn or rest house for travellers.

Below: Cycling in Nonsuch Park.

Starting Points: Stoneleigh station (1A) or any of the car parks (1B, 1C, 1D).

Parking: Three car parks — two off the A24 (London Road), the other off the A232 (Ewell Road).

Public Transport: Stoneleigh station is on the Guildford and Dorking lines out of Waterloo and is served by frequent trains.

Above: Nothing remains of the original palace except three markers showing its main axis.

Links to Other Paths: None.

Distance: The park has some 4km (2½ miles) of cycle paths. It's about 1km (0.6 miles) away from Stoneleigh station.

Map: Explorer 161.

Surfaces and Gradients: Flat, metalled roads.

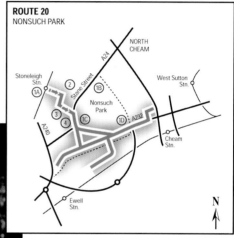

ROUTE 20
NONSUCH PARK

Roads and Crossings: Short road journey from the station but you must cross the A24, which can be busy.

Refreshments: Tea house in the park.

Route Instructions: 1A. From the station turn on to Broadway.

2. At the roundabout turn right on to Dell Road.

3. Then turn left on to Briarwood Road.

4. Turn right and cross the A24, entering the park at the car park 100yd

Left: London Cycling Campaign/Bob Allen

HAMPSTEAD HEATH

This is another short meander around a fascinating area of London. Until the 17th century the heath was thickly covered thorn and gorse common land owned by the lord of the manor. Today it is open parkland covering 170ha (420 acres) and a favourite picnic spot for Londoners. The heath first came to public attention as an area of clean air where Londoners could escape from the Great Plague. Later, at the beginning of the 18th century, the spring waters were claimed to have medicinal properties and Hampstead became something of a spa. John Constable lived in the village and often painted the heath.

The first real threat to its common status came in 1829 when its absentee lord of the manor, Thomas Maryon Wilson, repeatedly attempted to sell the heath for development. He even had much of the gorse cleared and planted rows of ornamental trees in preparation for residential streets, but he had to get a private Act of Parliament to enclose the land and build on it. Such a practice was a contemporary formality for commons all over the suburbs of London. Wilson attempted 10 bills in Parliament and each time was thwarted. He died in 1870 and the following year his son, who inherited the manor, sold 97ha (240 acres) to the Metropolitan Board of Works for £45,000.

Since then the heath has expanded fourfold: in 1886 109ha (270 acres) of Parliament Hill Fields were bought for £300,000; Golders Hill Park in 1899 for £38,000; Wildwood in 1904 for £43,000; finally, 81ha (200 acres) of Kenwood in 1927 came from the Iveagh Bequest. Now the Heath covers 334ha (825 acres). Unfortunately, not much of the park has permissible cyclepaths and so this figure-of-eight route has to take to the road occasionally.

Highgate Cemetery

Properly called the Cemetery of St James, inside these walls lie the remains of many remarkable people, including Michael Farraday, George Eliot, Dante Gabriel Rossetti, Christina Rossetti, Charles Dickens, Sir Ralph Richardson and, perhaps most famous of all, Karl Marx. Opened in 1839 by the London Cemetery Company on an 8ha (20-acre) site, it was built beside St Michael's church which was designed by the architect Lewis Vulliamy, in 1830. In its early days it was one of the most fashionable places to be seen dead. The landscape garden was laid out by David Ramsay, who devised serpentine roads and footpaths leading upwards towards the church.

Above: Cycling on the heath is strictly controlled with an 8mph speed limit and a shared cyclist/pedestrian path.
London Cycling Campaign/Bob Allen

Some wonderful Victorian tombs, epitaphs and statuary are to be found, but much of it is terribly overgrown. When it became full the cemetery was extended with the addition of the east side of Swain's Lane. On the west side lie the Egyptian avenue and the catacombs. Sadly, because it became very overgrown, the west cemetery was closed in 1975 as being too dangerous for public access. It has since been resurrected by volunteers but remains closed except for guided tours. The east cemetery (where Marx lies) is open still to the public but is very run down. It is nevertheless one of the most enchanting areas of London.

Kenwood House

The first house was built here around 1616, probably by the King's printer John Bull. In 1694 the then owner of Kenwood, William Brydges, rebuilt much of the house. It then changed hands a few times until bought in 1754 by William Murray, later the Chief Justice of the King's Bench and Earl of Mansfield. He commissioned the most popular contemporary interior designer, Robert Adam, and gave him a free rein to rebuild and redesign the house. Mansfield died in 1793 and his nephew, David Murray, hired George Saunders to add the two wings on the north façade. The house stayed in the family until 1922, when most of the estate (but not the house) was bought from the 6th Earl by the Kenwood Preservation Council to protect it from development by rapacious speculators. The land was opened to the public by London County Council in 1924. That same year Edward Guinness, 1st Earl of Iveagh, bought the remaining 30ha (74 acres) and Kenwood House which he filled with his extensive collection of paintings, including Rembrandt, Vermeer, Gainsborough and Stubbs. He presented the House and its remarkable contents to the nation before his death in 1927. The house was closed for the duration of World War 2, after which it became the responsibility of London County Council in 1949; it reopened to the public the following year.

Spaniards Inn

It's hard to miss Spaniards Inn: the road kinks round its weatherboarded sides. Built in 1585, the house is said to have acquired its name from when it was the Spanish ambassador,s official residence during the reign of James II. Its most notorious customer was Dick Turpin the highwayman who

Left: Hampstead Heath is an oasis of rural tranquillity in North London

stabled his horse, Black Bess, in the toll house opposite. In 1780 the landlord delayed the Gordon Rioters who were intent on torching Kenwood House (because the unpopular chief justice of the King's Bench, Lord Mansfield lived there) by plying them with drink until a detachment of soldiers arrived and disarmed them: their rifles are displayed in the saloon bar. The inn has been the meeting place for many famous patrons including Keats, Shelley, Byron and Dickens. Spaniards Inn also has a registered ghost, a grey lady.

Parliament Hill

Only 97.5m (320ft high), it nevertheless gives wonderfully impressive views over London, Highgate and Hampstead. Supposedly the other members of the Gunpowder Plot waited here to watch Parliament blow up in 1605, but instead Guy Fawkes was captured, arrested and tortured before being hung, drawn and quartered. In 1887 its 109ha (270 acres) were bought for $300,000 to preserve its open public status. It was a favourite spot with many poets and artists including Keats, Shelley, Leigh-Hunt and Coleridge. Nowadays kite flyers make up much of the crowd.

Starting Points: Jack Straw's Castle car park (1A), Hampstead Ponds car park (1B) or Hampstead Heath railway station (1C).

Parking: Hampstead Ponds car park or some street parking, but usually very busy.

Public Transport: Hampstead Heath railway station is on the North London Line from Richmond to North Woolwich.

Links to Other Paths:
2km (1¼ miles) from the Regent's Arm of the Grand Union.

Distance: Some 7–8km (c5 miles) of road and off-road cycling.

Map: Explorer 173.

Surfaces and Gradients: Some small hills but nothing too hard.

Roads and Crossings: Some road work and the A502 (North End Way/Heath Street) and B519 (Spaniards Road) have to be negotiated and crossed.

Refreshments:
Excellent places all round Hampstead including the Flask in Flask Walk, the Spaniards Inn towards Highgate and Jack Straws Castle.

Route Instructions: 1A. From the car park at Jack Straw's Castle cross to the edge of

the Heath along West Heath Road.
or
1B. From the Hampstead Ponds car park follow the edge of the Heath along East Heath Road. Cross over Heath Street and Spaniards Road on to the edge of the Heath along West Heath Road.
or
1C. Turn right out of Hampstead Heath railway station on to South End, which becomes East Heath Road. Follow the road to join the route at 2.

2. Proceed along the edge of the Heath next to West Heath Road until you reach the beginning of the cycle path adjacent to Platt's Lane.

3. Take the cycle path on to the Heath, running past Leg of Mutton Pond on your right and later a bandstand on your left, until you reach North End Road.

4. Turn right, and again using the edge of the Heath proceed down the North End Road side towards Jack Straw's Castle public house.

5. The cycle path picks up again on Spaniards Road just before it bisects North End Road and wends its way over the East Heath, past the Viaduct fishing pond. A clearly marked left fork then takes you across the main Heath between the Model Boating Pond and Highgate Men's Bathing

Pond to the Highgate side of the Heath on Millfield Lane.

6. Now turn right and follow the Heath down past the Highgate Men's Bathing Pond, Highgate Number 1 Pond and some tennis courts until you reach the cycle path again on the Highgate Road side of the Heath.

7. Taking the cycle path once more, go along the lower reaches of Parliament Hill past an area containing various amenities, including toilets and refreshments, a Park Office and another bandstand, a bowling

green, cricket and football pitches and an athletics track, until you reach the other side, near a children's playground. Now leave the park briefly and proceed straight down Nassington Road until it enters Parliament Hill. Take the left route past South Hill Park until you rejoin the Heath again. On your left opposite the Heath is Hampstead Heath railway station.

8. Crossing the Heath by Hampstead Pond Number 1 you can reach the car park at (1A) again. You can now cycle between the Hampstead Ponds.

9. Following the cycle path as it turns left, rejoin the main path across the East Heath to return to the car park at Jack Straw's Castle.

ROUTE 21
HAMPSTEAD HEATH

④

⑤ ⑥

West
Heath
③
(1A)

②   Hampstead
Ponds   Parliament Hill
⑨

⑦

⑧

N
↑   (1B)

(1C)
o Hampstead
Heath Stn.

Below: Cycling off the marked paths is expressly forbidden on Hampstead Heath. If you want to cycle in fields go to Epping!

ROUTE 22

HYDE PARK, GREEN PARK AND ST JAMES'S PARK

This is a fine route that shows off the centre of London from Trafalgar Square to the wonderfully restored Albert Memorial. It's best undertaken — like so much London cycling — on a Sunday morning so that you can enjoy the oddities of Speakers Corner. The route can be easily extended by road into Trafalgar Square and the National Gallery, or to the big Kensington museums but best of all you get to see three beautiful London parks, some amazing bronzes (on the Royal memorial) and even, if you're lucky, a flamingo or two!

PLACES OF INTEREST

Hyde Park

The largest of the central London parks at over 137ha (340 acres), it stretches from Bayswater Road in the north to Knightsbridge in the south. Park Lane is the eastern boundary and Kensington Gardens the western. The land belonged at one time to the monks of Westminster Abbey, but after the Dissolution of the Monasteries (1536) Henry VIII seized the lands, sold off some and kept the piece called Hyde which he fenced in for deer hunting (hunting continued until 1768). Queen Elizabeth also liked to hunt here and started the tradition of holding military reviews.

First opened to the public in 1637, the park quickly became fashionable. During the Civil War in 1642 it was requisitioned by the Parliamentarians (Roundheads) and trench fortifications (including a couple of forts) were built to keep out the Royalists (Cavaliers). In 1652 the park was divided into three lots and sold by order of Parliament for a total of £17,000. But at the Restoration in 1660 Charles II reclaimed the park, enclosed it with a brick wall and reopened it to the public. It again became a fashionable place to meet and promenade. But in common with all large open spaces in London it was also the haunt of highwaymen and vagabonds. Consequently, when William III came to live at Kensington Palace he ordered that 300 lamps be hung from the trees between Kensington Palace and St James's along the route du roi (now Rotten Row) thus becoming the first road in England to be lit at night. The highwaymen, however, continued to ply their trade there. Despite the threat of violence the park remained a highly fashionable gathering place for promenades and entertainments and for horse riding.

In 1730, on orders from Queen Caroline, William Kent supervised work on digging the lake now known as the Serpentine along the boggy watercourse of the River Westbourne. When finished it was 12m (40ft) deep and 1.6km (1 mile) long, with the grounds around being landscaped. In the 19th century the various lodges and gates were added, and the Victorians added many statues and monuments. For the Great Exhibition in 1851 Joseph Paxton's magnificent Crystal Palace was built between Rotten Row and the Knightsbridge Barracks. Over the next six months, over six million people visited the exhibition. The enormous profits went towards the building of the museums in Exhibition Road and the dismantling of the Crystal Palace and its re-erection at Sydenham.

Below: **Hyde Park.** *A.N.T. Photographics*

Speakers Corner, established by the Reform League, became a venue (on Sundays) for any persons with a grievance to lawfully speak their mind providing they are not obscene, blasphemous or inciting a breach of the peace.

Sheep grazed in the park until 1939. In 1960 the park lost 8.5ha (21 acres) for the widening of Park Lane — despite vociferous public protests. Until the onset of Dutch Elm Disease in the 1970s over 9,000 elms graced the park.

Kensington Gardens

Having briefly belonged to Henry VIII, this area was the private land of the Earl of Nottingham until 1689 when it and Nottingham House were bought for £18,000 by William III. The latter commissioned the architects Wren, Hawksmoor, Vanbrugh and Kent to transform the building into Kensington Palace. Queen Caroline created the gardens by supervising the landscaping and planting of a long avenue of trees and the making of the Round Pond. Kensington Palace remained the premier royal residence until 1790 when the gardens were opened to the genteel public (no soldiers, sailors or servants). Princess Victoria lived in the palace until she became queen and in 1840, after she left, the gardens were opened every day for whoever wished to enjoy them.

The most famous statue in the grounds is of Peter Pan by George Frampton. It was erected in 1912 beside the Long Water.

Below: Round Pond, Kensington Gardens. *A.N.T. Photographics*

Albert Memorial

This amazing extravagance in high Gothic taste sums up Victorian ideals and pretensions. Magnificently and expensively restored by English Heritage in time for the Millennium, it is well worth pausing to study. Revealed in early spring 1999 after years under plastic sheeting, the huge 53m (175ft-high) Albert Memorial is back to its former glory; it was designed by Gilbert Scott as a lasting tribute to Queen Victoria's consort. The memorial was finished in 1876 and paid for by public subscription plus a grant from Parliament (the Irish refused to contribute) and cost £120,000. The gilded bronze statue of Prince Albert is 4.2m (14ft high) and shows him seated, reading the catalogue of the Great Exhibition of 1851. The canopy is inlaid with mosaics, enamels, marbles and polished stone. There are seven tiers of statuary rising from the base. At each corner are marble groupings depicting Asia, Africa, Europe and America. On plinths at the corners of the podium are homages to Agriculture, Commerce, Engineering and Manufacture. The base has a marble frieze showing 169 life-size world-renowned figures from the arts — poets and musicians, painters, architects and sculptors. On the pillars are bronze statues of Astronomy, Chemistry, Geology, Geometry; in niches above are Rhetoric, Medicine, Philosophy and Physiology. On the spires are gilt bronze figures of Faith, Hope, Charity, Humility, Prudence, Justice, Fortitude and Temperance.

Green Park

The park is a triangle of 21ha (53 acres) between Piccadilly and Constitution Hill and is the smallest of the royal parks. Local legend has it that this was the burial ground for lepers from the hospital of St James's and that is why no flowers grow here. Originally enclosed by Henry III, it was made into a royal park by Charles II for use as a picnic area. To keep the royal wine chilled an ice box was dug; this was filled with snow in winter and covered with straw. As with all London parks it was a haunt of duellists and highwaymen. The River Tyburn (now

Above: **The gilded bronze statue of Prince Albert.**
A.N.T. Photographics

culverted) flows under the park. Constitution Hill was the scene for a number of assassination attempts — no less than three on Queen Victoria, and one on Edward VII.

Pall Mall

Named after an Italian croquet-like ball game called pallo a maglio, which was particularly popular with Charles II and his court. The road was built between two lines of elms to link St James's Palace and Charing Cross and named Catherine Street after Queen Catherine of Braganza, but the popular name stuck. From the first it was a fashionable and highly sought-after address. The king's mistress, Nell Gwyn, had a house at No 79 on the only non-Crown-owned ground on the south side — King Charles had given her the freehold in 1676 for services rendered. By the beginning of the 18th century expensive shops had opened along the road which became renowned for its coffee houses, many of which later developed into gentlemen's clubs such as Brook's, Boodle's, the Guards and the Marlborough.

Buckingham Palace

The Palace was built by George IV who demolished his parents' London house — Buckingham House (built 1702–5) — and after much delay and argument appointed John Nash (in 1825) as his architect. The House of Commons had authorised £200,000 for the improvement and repair of the original building but the king had much grander ideas — he wanted a completely new building made of Bath stone. Costs inevitably overran as George's extravagance took hold. The final bill was around £700,000 and even then it was finished only after George's death. Nash was dismissed in 1830 and in 1837 construction started again under the guidance of Edward Blore who completed the work, which included moving Nash's triumphal Marble Arch from the entrance to the courtyard to its present site. When Victoria came to the throne in 1837 the palace was only just habitable, with faulty drains, inadequate sanitation and thousands of windows which would not open at all. But Victoria was very happy there. The east front was replaced in 1913 with a Portland stone façade designed by Aston Webb.

Inside there are about 600 rooms linked by several miles of corridors, of which the Queen has a suite of about 12 on the first floor of the north wing overlooking Green Park. The Palace gardens cover 18ha (45 acres) and the only time the public gets to see them is during the summer garden parties held by the queen; when she is in residence her Royal Standard flies from the masthead.

Number One, London

Apsley House, now the Wellington Museum, was built between 1771-8 by Robert Adam for the Lord Chancellor, Henry, Earl of Bathurst. It is known as Number One, London for being the first house past the tollgate into London from the country. In 1817, after his great military career, Wellington took over the house from his brother and considerably extended it, making it much grander in the French style. The brick walls were faced with Bath stone

(brought up the Thames via the Kennet & Avon Canal) and the Corinthian portico was added. The 7th Duke of Wellington presented the house to the nation; it opened as the Wellington Museum in 1952. It houses a large and fine collection of paintings, furnishings and trophies as well as memorabilia of the Iron Duke. The house was extensively restored from 1992–5.

Royal Artillery War Memorial
Widely acknowledged as one of the most poignant war memorials anywhere, the massive Portland stone block base was designed by Lionel Pearson and is decorated with bas-reliefs of gunners. It is topped by a

Above: **Apsley House seen from the Hyde Park corner roundabout.** *A.N.T. Photographics*

9.2in howitzer, of which the angle of elevation is such that a shell fired from the barrel would reach the bloody battlefield of the Somme in northern France where so many Royal Artillerymen died. The four larger-than-life-size bronze figures were the work of Charles Sargeant Jagger. There is one on each side and on the north lies a dead soldier, beneath which is the roll of honour commemorating the 49,076 RA soldiers who died in the Great War of 1914-1918. The inscription reads: 'Here was a royal fellowship of death.'

Starting Points: Paddington station (1A), Waterloo station (1B).

Parking: Some meter parking in the area but it is always very busy.

Public Transport: West of England trains run into Paddington; Birdcage Walk (7) is quite easily reached from Waterloo station.

Links to Other Paths: Links to Route 5 at the Thames.

Distance: 1.5km (1 mile) to Waterloo, 0.5km (¼ mile) from Paddington; c10km (6 miles) round trip.

Map: Explorer 173.

Surfaces and Gradients: No gradients to speak of; the surfaces are all on road or purpose-built path.

Roads and Crossings: Road from the stations; Hyde Park Corner (by underpass); some of this route is on road and — apart from official cyclepaths — cycling is not permitted in the Royal Parks.

Refreshments: Too many to mention: there are a lot of kiosks in the parks and many good pubs nearby, particularly in Kensington.

Route Instructions: 1A. From Paddington turn right on to Praed Street then left on to Spring Street.
or
1B. Come out of Waterloo station by the main entrance and walk down the hill, turning left on to York Road. Cross Westminster Bridge and take Great George Street off Parliament Square. This leads to Birdcage Walk. Join the circuit at point (7).

2. Go right at Sussex Gardens and follow the road round on to Westbourne Street. Walk the bike across the busy A40 (Bayswater Road) and turn into Hyde Park on the North Carriage Ring.

3. Turn left and continue round to Speakers Corner and then cycle down to Hyde Park Corner.

4. Take the underpass into Constitution Hill, taking the opportunity to visit the Royal Artillery War Memorial and Constitution or Wellington Arch.

5. Turn left on to The Mall in front of Buckingham Palace and continue down to Admiralty Arch and Trafalgar Square.

6. Turn right down Horseguards Road and . . .

7. . . . at the bottom turn right into Birdcage Walk.

8. Go back up Constitution Hill, under Hyde Park Corner . . .

9 . . . and turn left to cycle along Rotten Row (note the Queen Mother's decorative 90th birthday gates).

10. Enjoy the renovated Albert Memorial and then either head south by road to see the Royal Albert Hall and the big museums (Science, Natural History and V&A) or . . .

11. . . . . retrace your path back to West Carriage Drive, turning left to complete the circuit.

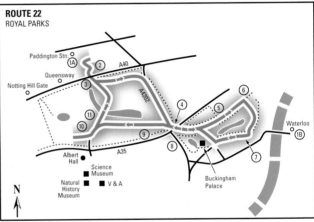

ROUTE 22
ROYAL PARKS

Below: **Albert Memorial.**
A.N.T. Photographics

BATTERSEA PARK

This is another gentle cycle ride for beginners and young families — it's short but there are interesting things to see in the park. First known as Battersea Fields, the common fields of the manor of Battersea, the Thames was roughly embanked here around 1560 and in 1671. Colonel Blood hid in the reeds with the intention of assassinating the bathing Charles II. The fields were notorious for their villains, riff-raff, gypsies and ne'er-do-wells, many of whom were attracted by the Red House Tavern. The great Duke of Wellington fought an illegal duel here in 1829 against the Earl of Winchelsea: both of them revoked, however, so nobody got hurt.

The fields became a park between 1846, when work began, and 1858, when John Gibson's 80ha (198-acre) design opened to the public. It is said that a million cubic feet of soil were used to

raise the land, which Gibson sculpted into walks, parterres, hills, waterfalls, lakes and, particularly, flowerbeds. Other gardening features include a Herb Garden, an Old English Garden begun in 1912, and two nature reserves — the Meadow and the Wilderness. The huge lake was designed by James Pennethorne and John Gibson during the 1860s and has three islands. The Cascades were built by John Pulham between 1866 and 1870 to give the impression of a geographical fault in sandstone rock. The Pump House, built to supply water from a well to the Cascades and lake, is used as an art gallery and information centre. One of the main centres for the 1951 Festival of Britain, today visitors can enjoy a riverside walk between Albert Bridge and Chelsea Bridge with views across the River Thames to Chelsea. There are many sculptures in the park — the most important are Henry Moore's 'Three Standing Figures', Eric Kennington's '24th Division' war memorial, and Barbara Hepworth's memorial to Dag Hammerskjold — 'Single Form'. On 18 May 1985, the Peace Pagoda erected by the Japanese Buddhist Order Nipponzan Myohoji was officially opened.

PLACES OF INTEREST

Battersea Bridge

Anyone coming here especially to see the Battersea Bridge of Whistler's paintings and drawings will be disappointed: that bridge was demolished in 1881 and replaced by the current one. The original bridge replaced the ferry service that plied between Chelsea and Battersea. The current bridge was designed by Sir Joseph Bazalgette and built between 1886-90 with five cast iron arches.

Left: Extend the route outside Battersea Park by crossing Battersea Bridge.
London Cycling Campaign/Tony Annis

Chelsea Bridge

Built in 1934, this suspension bridge by Rendel, Palmer and Tritton replaced an earlier suspension bridge.

Albert Bridge

Undoubtedly one of the prettiest bridges in London when lit up at night by the thousands of light bulbs, with their reflections rippling in the waters of the Thames. This three-span suspension bridge was built in 1871–3 by R. M. Ordish.

Battersea Power Station

The somewhat battered subject of a long on-going controversy, Battersea Power Station stopped working in 1983. Too big for any obvious use, but too architecturally valuable to demolish, this now listed building lies semi-destroyed while its future is debated. It was designed by Sir Giles Gilbert Scott as one of three great power stations to provide electricity for London (the others were at Kingston, now demolished, and Southwark, currently being converted into an extension of the Tate Gallery). It originally had two 91m

(300ft)-high chimneys but this was later doubled to increase capacity.

Royal Hospital, Chelsea

Founded by Charles II in 1682 for retired war veterans, the first 476 of whom arrived in 1689; the Royal Hospital building was designed and built by Sir Christopher Wren in the form of three quadrangles following rough plans drawn up by the diarist and courtier John Evelyn. It took 10 years to complete, by which time William III was on the throne and was subsequently altered and expanded over the years, including some work done by Robert Adam and Sir John Soane. In 1852 the Great Hall was used for the lying-in-state of the Duke of Wellington and thousands came to pay their last respects. The Hospital was badly bomb-damaged during the war and has largely been rebuilt.

The hospital grounds lead down to the Thames. This site now hosts the annual Chelsea Flower Show for four days of horticultural pandemonium and hype every May. The Hospital still gives a home to approximately 400 war veterans, known as Chelsea Pensioners, who have fallen on hard times. They have to be from the ranks and at least 65 years old and receive an allowance for 'beer and tobacco' from the state. In return Pensioners attend military church services and parades and on high days and holidays the Pensioners wear a smart, distinctive bright-red tunic designed in the late 18th century as a mark of their status.

Further down Royal Hospital Road lies the National Army Museum which opened in 1971 after the collection was moved from the Royal Military Academy, Sandhurst. The collection commemorates and celebrates the history of the British Army from 1485 — the beginning of the reign of Henry VII — onwards. It covers the military build-up of empire, colonisation and decline, as well as the growth of the regiments and their actions. Further west is the Chelsea Physic Garden.

Left: **Peace Pagoda in Battersea Park.**

Starting Points: Car park (1A) on Carriage Drive North, off the A3220 (Queenstown Road); Battersea Park railway station (1B).

Parking: Car park on Carriage Drive North.

Public Transport: Battersea Park railway station is just out of Victoria. Queenstown Road is only slightly further south.

Links to Other Paths: Putney Bridge and Route 4 is about 4km (2½ miles) west.

Distance: c7km (c4½ miles) with extensions.

Map: Explorer 161.

Surfaces and Gradients: Flat tarmac.

Roads and Crossings: Only if you come by train or cross Chelsea Bridge to visit the Royal Hospital, National Army Museum or Chelsea Physic Garden.

Refreshments: Facilities in the park; nice pub — the Prince Albert — on Parkgate Road off Albert Bridge Road.

Route Instructions: 1A. Circuit clockwise or anti-clockwise — but do not stray on to pedestrian areas.

ROUTE 23
BATTERSEA PARK

Royal Hospital
A3031
National Army Museum
Chelsea Bridge A3216
Chelsea Physic Garden
Albert Bridge
A3220
Embankment R.Thames
Chelsea
2
Battersea Bridge
1A
Battersea Park Stn.
N
3
1B
A3031
Battersea Church
BATTERSEA

or

1B. Follow the Queenstown Road towards Chelsea Bridge and turn left into the park.

2. Extend the route by crossing Chelsea Bridge and turning left off Chelsea Bridge Road on to Royal Hospital Road. Cross back at the Albert Bridge.

3. Extend the route eastwards along the Thames (although much of this is footpath) to St Mary's Church, Battersea, a most attractive Georgian church in which William Blake was married.

Left: London Cycling Campaign/ Jez Coulson/Insight

ROUTE 24

FINSBURY PARK TO HIGHGATE

To the west of Finsbury Park lies the old route of the Great Northern Railway. This now disused stretch of line runs between Finsbury Park and Highgate through cuttings and along high embankments. It has been moved to Parkland Walk.

PLACES OF INTEREST

Highgate Wood

Today a tiny remnant (20ha [70 acres]) of the old forest which once filled the London basin, the other pieces of which still exist in Holland Park and Epping Forest. The land and its magnificent beeches on the northeastern slopes of Highgate village were acquired in 1885 by the Corporation of London specifically to protect the ancient woodland and give Londoners access to open ground. It is kept as nearly as possible to its natural state.

Finsbury Park

Originally part of Hornsey Wood and owned by the Bishop of London, Finsbury Park was created by the Finsbury Park Act of 1857 to cater for the overcrowded citizens of the old borough of Finsbury some three miles to the southwest. It was bought at a cost of £472 per acre. The subsequent residential neighbourhood which grew up around the park became known as Finsbury Park. The park is an unremarkable 46.5ha (115 acres) with football pitches, a cricket ground and practice nets, a running track, a small lake and the American Gardens.

Starting Point: Finsbury Park railway station.

Parking: There's on-street parking in the area but, as with all of London, it can be difficult to find.

Public Transport: Finsbury Park station has frequent services. Crouch End station is about halfway along the route.

Links to Other Paths: Quite close (3km [2 miles]) to Hampstead and can be joined to Route 21 by road.

Distance: 6–7km (c4 miles) round trip.

Map: Explorer 173.

Surfaces and Gradients: Good trackway and tarmac.

Roads and Crossings: None.

Refreshments: Finsbury Park is a busy shopping area with many possibilities for refreshments. (The area is also extremely busy when Arsenal FC have a home game.)

Route Instructions: 1. From the Finsbury Park entrance at the bottom of Stroud Green Road, just before the railway bridges, follow the gravel track as it spirals up from the ornamental gateway to the height of the railway. The route then follows the active railway on its left, with Finsbury Park behind a fence on the right.

Left: The Stroud Green Road entrance to the Parkland Way.

2. Shortly, ¼–½-mile later the track comes out at a crossroads, with a pedestrian footbridge over the active railway lines to the left and an entrance to the park on the right. Cross over the footbridge and take the turning immediately to the right to start on the track proper.

3. The route follows the trackbed of the old railway, past a couple of old platforms and across various bridges over the local main roads. At times this is quite densely wooded, at others there are vistas of north London; it ends at the huge dual tunnels of Highgate Hill. These are barred, gated and locked, home to derelicts and exuding a somewhat sinister feeling. Beyond them is only a ghostly Highgate station.

4. The Highgate exit is on the left, where a discernible track and gate open on to Holmsdale Road.

Above: Reflective strips and bright jackets ensure visibility at night and in bad weather. *London Cycling Campaign/ Suzanne Janson*

Below: A dull afternoon on the Parkland Way — but still better than sitting at home!

ROUTE 24
FINSBURY PARK – HIGHGATE
(Following the disused railway line)

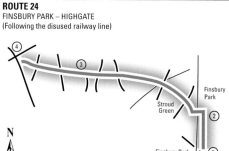

Finsbury Park

Stroud Green

Finsbury Park Stn.

N

WHITEWEBBS COUNTRY PARK, TRENT COUNTRY PARK AND HADLEY WOOD

Off-road in the countryside near Enfield, this is a pretty demanding route. Nevertheless, that's why you bought a mountain bike, so don't moan! There's a bit of road and a short detour allows a visit to Forty Hall — unfortunately not the author's family estate! This route is certainly worth doing on a good day — and has a number of escape points if time is getting on. If you want to take it easy, split it into two segments: first from Enfield Lock station or Forty Hall car park to Whitewebbs Park and back via Forty Hall; second from Oakleigh Park station or Trent Country Park car park up the Cockfosters Road and then around the Hadley Wood and Trent circuit.

PLACES OF INTEREST

Enfield Chase

This is the remains of the once-huge ancient royal hunting forest of Enfield Chase, bits of which have been given away or sold off over the centuries. It originally became Crown property in 1399 when the Duke of Lancaster (later Henry IV) married Mary de Bohun who brought the Chase as her dowry, the whole then being incorporated into the Duchy of Lancaster. The Chase remained a royal hunting preserve until 1777 when by an Act of Parliament it was enclosed and parcels of land portioned off to local parishes. The central 121ha (300 acres) were retained by the Crown but let out on 99-year leases for agricultural development. However, the land was generally not farmed successfully and much of it was built on instead, in the process creating the housing estate of Hadley Wood. Most of the houses have covenants on them and the Duchy still retains a number of freeholds.

Trent Country Park

The royal physician Dr Richard Jebb was given 81ha (200 acres) of Enfield Chase in gratitude for saving the life of the Duke of Gloucester (King George III's brother) at Trento in the Austrian Tyrol. Following generations added 283ha (700 acres) to the holding and vastly improved the house and gardens. On the death of Sir Philip Sassoon in 1939 the house was requisitioned by the government and subsequently used as an interrogation centre for enemy airmen. Postwar, in 1952 the estate became the possession of Middlesex County Council. The mansion itself and the surrounding 81ha (200 acres) became a teacher training college.

Forty Hall

Between 1609 and 1613 a canal — the New River — was built to bring water from Hertfordshire to the City of London. The line almost followed the course of the Lea but diverted into side valleys to lessen the gradient and reduce the

Left: Bridleways can usually be cycled but beware hardened hoofprints: you can get badly jarred if you're not careful.

speed of flow. This water course almost encircled Forty Hall until between 1853–6 the New River was straightened out, but a loop survives in the grounds of the Hall. Forty Hall was built between 1629 and 1636 for Sir Nicholas Rainton, a wealthy haberdasher and one-time Lord Mayor of London. It is built in what has been called the 'artisan mannerist' style, a term for a mish-mash of Elizabethan and Jacobean styling favoured by wealthy merchants of the area. Much of the building retains its original interior including panelling, ceilings and chimney pieces. The Hall was sold to Enfield Council in 1951 by the last private owner, Derek Parker Bowles; it is now used as a museum.

Hadley Wood

On the extreme west of Enfield Chase lies the large estate known as Hadley Wood. This has grown up over the last century as a secure middle-class suburb. It came about after 1850 when the Great Northern Railway main line from the north into London cut through the most westerly section of Enfield Chase. It was started by leaseholder Charles Jack who successfully negotiated with the railway to build a station on the land, around which he agreed to build an estate. The station opened in 1884 and 50 houses were built. The agreement between the Duchy and Jack ended acrimoniously in 1941 when some land and freeholds were sold. When a degree of prosperity returned to the country after the war, two decades of intensive building of private houses transpired. Today it has a pleasant feeling of *rus in urbe* and houses are highly sought after.

Starting Points: Enfield Lock (1A) or Oakleigh Park railway stations (1B), Trent Country Park car park (1C)— if (1B), do the route the other way round.

Parking: The country parks have parking facilities.

Public Transport: Good rail services from Liverpool Street to Enfield Lock, and from King's Cross or Moorgate to Oakleigh Park (en route to Welwyn Garden City).

Links to Other Paths: Links to Route 15 at Enfield Lock.

Distance: c25km (c15 miles) from station to station including a detour to Forty Hall.

Map: Explorer 173.

Surfaces and Gradients: Some busy roads, some tough off-road tracks.

Roads and Crossings: Quite a lot of road but this is made up for by the off-road sections. It is quite easy just to do Trent Country Park or Hadley Common if you want to limit your roadwork.

Refreshments: The country parks have facilities as do Cockfosters and Barnet.

Route Instructions:

1A. Turn right out of Enfield Lock railway station and take Bradley Road down to the Prince of Wales footpath (2).
or
1B. If you start from the station either do the route in reverse or curtail it to the Hadley Wood and Trent Country Park section.
or
1C. If you start from the Trent Country Park car park, limit yourself to the Hadley Wood section. Turn right on to the A111 Cockfosters Road and join the route at (10).

3. Jink right (on to the A1010 Hertford Road) and then left on to Turkey Street.

4. At the T-junction turn left to visit Forty Hall. You can continue along this road (Forty Hill Road) and take Clay Hill Road at the roundabout, rejoining the route at (7).

5. Once the detour is over, continue along Bull's Cross until you turn left into Whitewebbs Lane.

6. Go past the pub (on the left) and car park (on the right). c2km (1¼ miles) after joining Whitewebbs Lane turn left on to the track that becomes Flash Lane.

7. Turn on to Strayfield Road in front of the church.

8. Turn left on to Rectory Farm Road bridlepath.

9. At the bottom cross the A1005 (The Ridgeway) and take Oak Avenue to turn right on to Hadley Road.

10. At the A111 Cockfosters Road jink right and then left on to Beech Hill (which becomes Camlet Way) to go through Hadley Wood. (You can turn left here and rejoin the route at (13).)

11. Turn left at the T-junction on to Hadley Common and follow the Hadley Wood Road over the railway line and past Beech Hill Lake.

12. Follow Games Road at the end of the common, turning right on to Chalk Lane.

13. Cross the A111 once more and enter the southern part of Trent Country Park. (Or continue at (15).)

14. Do the circuit — a well-marked c4km (c2½ miles) route.

15. Go back to the A111; turn left and then right at the A110 (Cat Hill).

16. Follow this road, bearing left on the B193 at the fork with Brookhill Road.

17. Go left at the church on to Church Hill and then right at the school on to Capel Road that leads to the station.

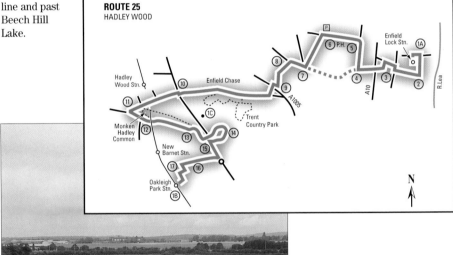

ROUTE 25
HADLEY WOOD

Left: It's hard to believe that you can get into the countryside so close to London.

EPPING FOREST

OK, it's a bit outside London, but Epping Forest has been the place to which East London has come at the weekend for so long that it demands inclusion in this book. Without doubt, of all the places you can go in London, this is the best for off-road cycling. The area is peaceful, attractive, offers brilliant views and super pubs. Its only drawback? A lot of people know it's there and the roads — and trackways — can get congested.

PLACES OF INTEREST

Epping Forest

Another remnant of the ancient forest which at one time stretched from the Thames to the Wash, Epping Forest has hidden almost as many secrets and witnessed as many events as English history can provide. Two Iron Age earthworks — Loughton Camp and Ambersbury Banks — remain in the forest, the latter reputed to be the site of Queen Boudicca's last stand against the Romans. The forest was for many centuries a favourite royal hunting ground; Queen Elizabeth even built her own lodge at Chingford from which to survey the hunt. Until the beginning of the 18th century the public were forbidden to hunt in the park except on Easter Monday. This exception was granted to citizens of London by Henry III in 1226 and the event became a big annual festival until it was stopped around 1882, by which time it had become an excuse for mayhem. From the 18th century after the relaxation of strict laws restricting access to the forest the area was used by travellers and highwaymen — even William III was almost kidnapped here. By the mid-18th century the forest was shrinking through increasing enclosures, until by 1851 there were only 2,428ha (6,000 acres) unenclosed, and even this was halved 10 years later. The situation was so desperate that court action was needed, a ruling being made that all enclosures since 1851 were illegal and should be compulsorily repurchased, and an Act of Parliament in 1878 gave the remaining 6,000 acres to the Corporation of London for protection. In 1882 the forest was finally declared open to all-comers to enjoy in perpetuity. Today it is the lungs of London, and a splendid place to cycle.

Queen Elizabeth's Hunting Lodge

Built on top of a hill as a grandstand to enable spectators to watch the hunt sweep past below, Elizabeth I hunted around Epping Forest from this building and also liked to shoot deer from the galleries. The lodge was built in the early 16th century, at which time it had no outer walls.

Above: Queen Elizabeth's Hunting Lodge on the edge of Epping Forest.

Starting Points: Anywhere in the park provides interesting rides; most books give a variation of the route mentioned here, but there are good trails throughout the forest, including all the bits south of the A1069 (Ranger's Road) and Queen Elizabeth's Hunting Lodge.

Parking: There are car parks all over Epping Forest

Public Transport: The Underground runs down the eastern edge of the wood, the railway on the western side with Chingford station (1A) only a short (0.5km/c¼-mile) ride from Queen Elizabeth's Hunting Lodge. Chingford is served from London Liverpool Street.

Links to Other Paths: Enfield Lock is only 4km (2½ miles) away from (3) as the crow flies, so you can link with Route 15.

Distance: Up to you: depends on your fitness. This route is 8km (5 miles) long but can be easily extended.

Map: Explorer 174.

Surfaces and Gradients: Some tracks, some paths. Can be heavy going when damp!

Roads and Crossings: Short piece of road from the station; this route crosses the busy A104 (Epping New Road) a couple of times.

Refreshments: Café at High Beach; The King's Oak near the Conservation Centre; the Robin Hood on the A104 just south of the centre; tea rooms and a big pub at Queen Elizabeth's Hunting Lodge. The Tea Hut just up from the Robin Hood pub is a favourite meeting place for bikers (of the engined variety).

Route Instructions: 1A. Turn right out of Chingford station and cycle along the A1069 (Ranger's Road) for about 500m (c¼ mile).
or

1B. From the car park, cross the A1069 and take the Green Ride north. It joins the Centenary Walk crossing a metalled road (2) — go left to visit the pretty High Beach church or the tea hut — before reaching High Beach (3) and the Epping Forest Conservation Centre (tel: 020 8508 0028 — it provides information, maps, books, cards, displays and advice on the area).

4. From the Conservation Centre follow the Centenary Walk over the A104 and on to Clay Ride.

5. After 500m (¼ mile) turn right on to another Green Ride, going over Strawberry Hill and cross Earl's Path near a pond (6).

7. Fork right in front of the second of Strawberry Hill's ponds, crossing the A104 (8) and Fairmead Lane (9) at Fairmead Bottom.

10. Follow the track back to your starting point via Grimston's Oak, Connaught Water and Magpie Hill.

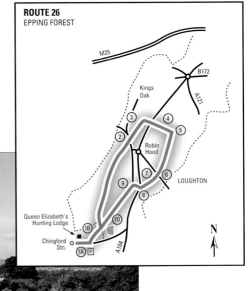

ROUTE 26
EPPING FOREST

Left: Epping Forest is an excellent place to cycle offroad.

GREENWICH, BLACKHEATH AND THE RAVENSBOURNE RIVER

This is another route that has a little more road work than is desirable, but maritime Greenwich is such a good day out that I have included it anyway. The National Maritime Museum — the largest maritime museum in the world — is the centrepiece of maritime Greenwich and was founded in 1937; it has recently been renovated. The Royal Naval College was commissioned by Queen Mary in 1694 and designed and built by Sir Christopher Wren and later Vanbrugh. After his death Vice-Admiral Lord Nelson was brought back to Greenwich and laid out in state in the Painted Hall of the Royal Naval College. However, almost the best thing about this route is the view from the Observatory over the Isle of Dogs on to London. The extension to the Ravensbourne River requires road cycling but the river path is worth it.

PLACES OF INTEREST

Blackheath

The black, acidic peaty soil of this common-land prevented its cultivation. At one time the very word Blackheath sent shivers of dread down the back of every traveller for its well-earned hazardous reputation, being for centuries the sinister haunt of ruthless highwaymen who preyed on travellers journeying between London, Canterbury and the Channel port of Dover.

The Romans built Watling Street across Blackheath and there were undoubtedly ancient walkways already across the heath. Those few highwaymen that were caught were left to hang on gibbets on Shooter's Hill to discourage their fellows and to remind the unwary of the dangers of the Heath. Only in the late 18th century did the Heath become relatively safe when it became a residential suburb.

With its wide, open spaces, Blackheath was used as the assembly point in June 1381 for the Peasants' Revolt led by Wat Tyler; Jack Cade's army camped overnight here in 1450; in 1415 Henry V was welcomed here after the Battle of Agincourt by the Lord Mayor and the court; it was the site of the 1497 battle between Henry VII and Michael Joseph and his Cornish rebels (they were buried in mass graves such as Whitfield's Mount); in 1540 Henry VIII met his bride-to-be Anne of Cleves here, and in 1660 Charles II was formally welcomed back to England on Blackheath. In the 18th century the Heath was used by the Revivalists Wesley and Whitefield for their meetings.

A fair has been held on the Heath every summer since 1689, when the first cattle fair was held. In 1608 the first golf club in England, the Royal Blackheath, was founded after James I showed how to play the game (it has since moved to Eltham), and the Blackheath Rugby Club is the oldest in Britain. In 1871 the 108ha (267 acres) left undeveloped by an expanding village were made into a public open space. Blackheath Gate is where the 20,000 runners in the annual London Marathon start their ordeal.

Queen's House

The house was built on land given to Anne of Denmark by James I in 1605. In 1616 Inigo Jones was commissioned to build a house but Anne died in 1619 before the building work had got far. Prince Charles inherited the building and gave it to his queen, Henrietta Maria, and asked Jones to finish the building. Starting in 1629, by 1640 had Jones produced a Palladian-style H-shaped building on either side of the Deptford to Woolwich road which passed through a bridge connecting the two sides. The queen was delighted with the work and it was dubbed 'The House of Delights'. In 1642 she lost the house to the Parliamentarians and they sold much of the surrounding land.

Royal Observatory

Several sites were proposed for the observatory including Hyde Park and Chelsea College (favoured by the Astronomer Royal, John Flamsteed) but Sir Christopher Wren championed Greenwich Park and Charles II agreed. The latter supplied £500 and bricks from Tilbury Fort and promised to pay for the instruments (although he later found reasons not to). The Circle Room in the Royal Observatory (built in 1674) contains the Airy Transit Circle whose longitudinal centre line (0° longitude) defines the Prime Meridian

of the world. Since 1767 and the publication of the British Nautical Almanack, British ships around the world used the Royal Observatory as their 'prime meridian' for navigation; other countries tended to measure time from their own capital cities. However, the Almanack was increasingly widely used by navigators of all nationalities. Then, in New York in 1884 at the International Congress, it was agreed that Greenwich Mean Time should become the official world standard so that from the Greenwich meridian line time around the globe is calculated as being plus or minus Greenwich Mean Time.

Cutty Sark

One of the last of the great fast tea clippers that plied the perilous trade route round the Cape of Good Hope all the way to China, she was built on the Clyde in 1869 and takes her name from Robbie Burns' poem *Tam o' Shanter* in which the witch Nannie wears a short shirt called a 'cutty sark'. The opening of the Suez Canal and the arrival of steam, with the consequent cutting of journey time spelled the end of this era. The *Cutty Sark* was rescued from destruction, restored and opened to the public in 1954. She has recently been extensively renovated. Inside she houses a magnificent collection of figureheads from vessels long gone as well as full-scale cabin replicas.

Left: **Entrance to the Greenwich Foot Tunnel.**

Below: **Cutty Sark.**

National Maritime Museum restaurant is also good and there are refreshment facilities at the Royal Observatory.

Route Instructions: 1A. From the station turn left on to the A206 (Greenwich High Road) and follow the road around on to Greenwich Church Street which leads down to the river.

Starting Points: Greenwich railway station (1A); parking at Greenwich (1B).

Parking: There are car parks and street parking in Greenwich (Park Row is convenient but busy) and a car park at the Barrier Visitors Centre.

Public Transport: Greenwich railway station is served by trains from Charing Cross, Waterloo East, Cannon Street and London Bridge.

Links to Other Paths: On the Isle of Dogs cycle along Westferry Road, Bow Street and Scott Street to reach the Limehouse Cut (Route 13). Route 7 goes west to Waterloo and Route 8 follows the river path east to the Thames Barrier.

Distance: 4–5km (c3 miles) round trip if you go back to the park at Vanbrugh Gate; another 7km (c4½ miles) if you go up Ravensbourne River to Lower Sydenham.

Map: Explorer 162.

Surfaces and Gradients: Good tarmac roadways.

Roads and Crossings: The road from the station is busy, as is the A206. Maze Hill, up the side of Greenwich Park, is usually quiet but the roads on Blackheath can get busy. The road route to the Ravensbourne is also busy.

Refreshments: Greenwich is full of pubs and other places to find refreshments, the Trafalgar by the Royal Naval College providing particularly good value. The

2. Cross by the Victorian foot tunnel (built 1902, it takes about 10 minutes to walk through the tunnel itself, plus a ride in the Victorian lifts at either end) to Island Gardens and walk along the river until you can look between the two arms of the Royal Naval College, up the hill to the Royal Observatory. You'll be looking the other way soon and it makes an interesting comparison. (If you want a good view of the Dome, cycle along Manchester Road to Cold Harbour where there are excellent views across the Thames.) Return to the south bank by the tunnel and make your way east along the river from Greenwich Pier, in front of the Royal Naval College to the Trafalgar pub.
or
1B. From Park Row car park it's best to do the route in reverse, going straight along the river to the foot tunnel.

3. From the Trafalgar go up Park Row, taking care when you cross the A206 (Trafalgar Road).

4. There's an entrance to the park here that you're not allowed to enter on bikes. Just inside and to the left, there's a boating lake and children's play area. If you have small children with you, it's sensible to enter the park here and push your bikes up to the Observatory.

5. Go along Park Vista and turn right on to Maze Hill. While not a particularly busy

road, there are so many cars parked along it that it can be tricky to negotiate the hill and keep an eye out for car doors, etc. Take care!

6. At Vanbrugh Gate enter the park and ride to Blackheath Avenue, taking the cycle route down to the crossroads turning on to Great Cross Avenue (7). Turn right at the intersection with Blackheath Avenue and check out the view from the Royal Observatory. Then retrace your steps, either carrying on up Blackheath Avenue and turning left and then right on to Prince Charles's Avenue (8) and rejoining the route at (11); or turn right (9) down The Avenue to St Mary's Gate at the bottom of the park (the National Maritime Museum restaurant is a short way to the right of this). Cross Stock Street on to Burney Street (10) and then turn right on to the B209 (Royal Hill) which joins the A206 (turn left) Greenwich High Street a short way from the station.

11. Go over the A2 (Shooters Hill Road) and turn right on to Montpelier Row.

12. Go past Blackheath railway station and turn right on to the B220 (Lee Terrace).

13. Cross the A20 (Lea Bridge) on to Lewis Grove and then take the busy A21 (Lewisham High Street) until you turn right on to Ladywell Road.

14. A short way up on the left is the entrance to a delightful 4km (2½ miles) of riverside with only one road to cross — the

Below: View down the Ravensbourne from an excellent curly-wurly bridge.

A205 (Catford Road), which you do by leaving Ladywell Fields, turning left on to Bourneville Road and then right on Adenmore Road. Cross the A205 and take the entrance to the next stretch of river. Alternatively, Catford railway station will take you back to London Bridge and Waterloo.

15. At the A2218 (South End Lane) either retrace your steps or cross the road and take Worsley Bridge Road to Lower Sydenham railway station.

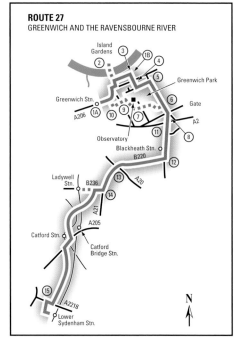

ROUTE 27
GREENWICH AND THE RAVENSBOURNE RIVER

APPENDICES

1. Sustrans

Architects of the National Cycle Network and the London Cycle Network.
All public enquiries should be addressed to the Bristol Head Office.

Head Office:
35 King Street
Bristol BS1 4DZ
Tel: 0117 926 8893
Public Information Line:
0117 929 0888
Press Office: 0117 927 4173
Website: www.sustrans.org.uk

Regional Offices:
Scotland:
3 Coates Place,
Edinburgh EH3 7AA
Tel: 0131 623 7600
Fax: 0131 623 7761

North East:
Rockwood House, Barn Hill,
Stanley Co Durham
DH9 8AN
Tel: 01207 281259
Fax: 01207 281113

Midlands:
St Paul's Community Centre
Hightown, Crewe CW1 3BY
Tel: 01270 211030
Fax: 01270 250683

East England:
33A Westgate,
Peterborough PE1 1PZ
Tel: 01733 319981
Fax: 01733 346902

South East England:
143 High Street
Lewes, East Sussex BN7 1XT
Tel: 01273 488190
Fax: 01273 488192

Thames, London and Kent:
14-16 Cowcross Street
Farringdon, London EC1M 6DR
Tel: 020 7336 8203
Fax: 020 7250 3022

South West England and Wales:
35 King Street
Bristol BS1 4DZ
Tel: 0117 926 8893
Fax: 0117 929 4173

Northern Ireland:
Room 403
McAvoy House
17A Ormeau Avenue,
Belfast BT2 8HD
Tel: 01232 434569
Fax: 01232 434556

2. LCC (The London Cycling Campaign)

The London Cycling Campaign aims to promote safe and fun cycling for all Londoners.
It produces its own magazine, a definitive guide for London cycling: *On Your Bike*, price £4.95
plus p+p= £5.70.

London Cycling Campaign
228 Great Guildford Business Square
30 Great Guildford Street, London SE1 0HS
Tel: 020 7928 7220 Website: www.sustrans.org.uk

3. London Cycle Network

Project Manager for the London Boroughs is John Lee, employed by the Royal Borough of
Kingston Upon Thames. He reports to the Steering Group (see below).

John Lee
Guildhall 2, Kingston Upon Thames, Surrey, KT1 1EU Tel: 020 8547 5917

4. London Cycle Steering Group

The London Cycle Steering Group is carrying forward the London Cycle Network on behalf of the
London boroughs. It includes those boroughs marked with an asterisk in Section 5 and the
organisations listed below.

London Cycle Steering Group
Mr K. Huggett Road Safety & Traffic Manager
Directorate of Environment Services
(Engineering & Transportation)
Royal Borough of Kingston Upon Thames
Guildhall 2 Kingston Upon Thames, Surrey KT1 1EU
Tel: 020 8547 4679 Fax: 020 8547 5926

Government Office for London
Mr P. Philippou
London Cycling Campaign
2 Marsham Street, London SW1P 3EB
Tel: 020 7276 6780
Fax: 020 7276 5198 or 5138

Highways Agency
Mr A. Mellors, St Christopher House, Southwark Street
London SE1 0TE Tel: 020 7921 4447 Fax: 020 7921 2364
London Cycling Campaign
Ms E. Church 3 Stamford Street, London SE1 9NT
Tel: 020 7928 7220 or 6112 Fax: 020 7928 2318

Sustrans (London Office)
Ms J. Hegett 14-16 Cowcross Street, London EC1 6DR
Tel: 020 7336 8203 Fax: 020 7250 3022

Traffic Control Systems Unit
Mr G. Ulph, Kings Building, Smith Square
London SW1P 3HQ Tel: 020 7343 5302 Fax: 020 7821 6744

Traffic Director for London
Mr D. Turner, College House, Great Peter Street,
London SW1P 3LN Tel: 020 7233 0045 Fax: 020 7976 8640

5. The London Boroughs:
Note: Personnel and addresses change regularly.

BARKING & DAGENHAM
Mike Lively, Borough Cycling Officer
London Borough of Barking & Dagenham
Civic Centre, Wood Street, Dagenham, Essex RM10 7BN
Tel: 020 8227 3110 Fax: 020 8594 8077

BARNET
Mr T. Sadiq, Directorate of Technical Services
London Borough of Barnet, Barnet House
1255 High Road Whetstone, London N20 0EJ
Tel: 020 8359 4457 Fax: 020 8359 4887

BEXLEY
Mr M. Sehmi, Traffic & Transportation Division
London Borough of Bexley, Sidcup Place
Sidcup, Kent DA14 6BT
Tel: 020 8303 7777 x3629 Fax: 020 8302 0263

BRENT
Mr R. Sainsbury, Engineering Client Services
London Borough of Brent, 5th Floor Brent House,
349-357 High Road Wembley, Middlesex HA9 6BZ
Tel: 020 8937 5077 Fax: 020 8900 5425

BROMLEY
Ms J. Awuah, Cycling Liaison Officer
London Borough of Bromley, Bromley Civic Centre,
Stockwell Close, Bromley, Kent BR1 3UH
Tel: 020 8313 4528 Fax: 020 8302 0263

CAMDEN
Mr G. Morris, Traffic Management Team
London Borough of Camden, Town Hall Extension,
Argyle Street, Camden , London WC1H 8EO
Tel: 020 7860 5898 Fax: 020 7860 5585

CITY OF LONDON
Mr I. Simmons, City Engineers Department
City of London, Guildhall, London EC2P 2EJ
Tel: 020 7332 1151 Fax: 020 7332 1559

CROYDON
Mr B. Williams, Highways & Traffic Section
London Borough of Croydon, Taberner House,
Park Lane, Croydon CR9 3RN
Tel: 020 8760 5425 Fax: 020 8760 5664

EALING
Mr D. Knowles, BRETS, London Borough of Ealing
24 Uxbridge Road, London W5 2BP
Tel: 020 8758 5272 Fax: 020 8758 8243

ENFIELD
Mr G. Ludlow, Cycling Officer, London Borough of Enfield
Civic Centre, Silver Street
Enfield, Middlesex EN1 2BP
Tel: 020 8967 9436 Fax: 020 8982 7405

GREENWICH
Mr R. Warhurst, Cycling Officer,
London Borough of Greenwich, Peggy Middleton House,
50 Woolwich New Road, London SE18 6QH
Tel: 020 8854 8888 Fax: 020 8316 6095

HACKNEY
Mr L. Mulrooney, London Borough of Hackney,
Traffic & Transportation
161-189 City Road, London EC1V 1NR
Tel: 020 7418 8221 Fax: 020 7418 8100

HAMMERSMITH & FULHAM
Mr S. Franklin
London Borough of Hammersmith & Fulham
Cycling Officer, Hammersmith Town Hall
King Street, London
Tel: 020 8748 3020 x3353 Fax: 020 8741 5664

HARINGEY
Mr C. BainbridgeCycling Officer,
London Borough of Haringey, Room 5, Hornsey Town Hall,
The Broadway, Crouch End, London N8 9JJ
Tel: 020 8862 1767 Fax: 020 8862 1742

HARROW
Mr J. Lee, Forward Planning — Planning Division
London Borough of Harrow, PO Box 37
Civic Centre, Station Road, Harrow, London HA1 2UY
Tel: 020 8863 5611 Fax: 020 8424 1551 or 1006

HAVERING
Mr M. Karin, Transport & Engineering,
London Borough of Havering, Spilsby Road, Romford,
Essex RM3 8UU
Tel: 01708 772804 Fax: 01708 773766

HILLINGDON
Mr H. A. Castelijn, Joint Transportation Group
London Borough of Hillingdon, Civic Centre, High Road
Uxbridge, Middlesex UB8 1UW
Tel: 01895 250 841 Fax: 01895 250 830

HOUNSLOW
Mr S. Sishu, Planning & Transportation Department
London Borough of Hounslow, Civic Centre
Lampton Road, Hounslow, Middlesex TW3 4DN
Tel: 020 8862 5453 Fax: 020 8862 5801

ISLINGTON
Mr R. Muruhathasan, Head of Planning Department
London Borough of Islington, 227/228 Essex Road
Islington, London N1
Tel: 020 7477 2817 Fax: 020 7477 2134

KENSINGTON & CHELSEA
Mr W. Mount, Highways & Traffic Department
Royal Borough of Kensington & Chelsea, Town Hall
Hornton Street, London W8 7NX
Tel: 020 7361 2736 Fax: 020 7938 5478

KINGSTON UPON THAMES
Mr J. Martin, Directorate of Environment Services
(Engineering & Transportation)
Royal Borough of Kingston Upon Thames
Guildhall 2, Kingston Upon Thames, Surrey KT1 1EU
Tel: 020 8547 5917 Fax: 020 8547 5926

LAMBETH
Mr M. Kahn, Transportation Planning Section
London Borough of Lambeth, George West House
2 Clapham Common North, London SE6 4RY
Tel: 020 7926 7100 Fax: 020 7926 7426 or 7155

LEWISHAM
Mr B. Dalton, Transportation Planning Group
London Borough of Lewisham, Deptford Town Hall
PO Box 927, London SE14 6AP
Tel: 020 8695 6000 x5013 Fax: 020 8469 2715

MERTON
Mr P. Thomas, Environmental Studies
London Borough of Merton, Merton Civic Centre
London Road, Morden, Surrey SM4 5DX
Tel: 020 8543 3192 Fax: 020 8543 6085

NEWHAM
Mr M. Hill, Technical Services, Engineering Division
London Borough of Newham, 25 Nelson Street, London
E6 4EH Tel: 020 8472 1430 x22370 Fax: 020 8472 1815

REDBRIDGE
Mr. J Redman,, Borough Cycling Officer
London Borough of Redbridge, PO Box 2,
128-142 High Road, Ilford, Essex IG1 1DD
Tel: 020 8478 3020 Fax: 020 8478 9115

RICHMOND
Ms C. Rapley, London Borough of Richmond on Thames
Civic Centre, 44 York Street, Twickenham, Middlesex
TW1 3BZ Tel: 020 8891 7310 Fax: 020 8891 7702

SOUTHWARK
Mr A. Barkatoolah, Engineering & Public Works
London Borough of Southwark, Municipal Offices
Larcom Street, London SE17 1RY
Tel: 020 7525 2056 Fax: 020 7525 2059

SUTTON
Mr K. Fraser, Technical Services Department
London Borough of Sutton, 24 Denmark Road
Carshalton, Surrey SM5 2JG
Tel: 020 8770 6524 Fax: 020 8770 6112

TOWER HAMLETS
Mr M. Hickford (Transportation)
London Borough of Tower Hamlets
Mulberry Place, 5 Clove Crescent, London E14 2BG
Tel: 020 7364 5000 x4803 Fax: 020 7364 4919

WALTHAM FOREST
Ms G. Harkell, Development Department
London Borough of Waltham Forest, Municipal Offices
The Ridgeway, London E4 6PS
Tel: 020 8527 5544 Fax: 020 8524 8960

WANDSWORTH
Mr M. Raisebeck/Mr S. Khan, Borough Engineers Depnt
London Borough of Wandsworth, Town Hall
(Municipal Building), Wandsworth High Street London
SW18 2PU Tel: 020 8871 6570 Fax: 020 8871 6670

WESTMINSTER
Mr P. McBride, Transport Policy, Westminster City Council
City Hall, Victoria Street, London SW1E 6QP
Tel: 020 7798 3171 Fax: 020 7798 2665

6. Bicycle Association
Produces a set of information sheets and leaflets for new cyclists. Send a 38p sae to:
Bicycle Association, Starley House, Eaton Road, Coventry CV1 2FHTel: 024 7655 3838

7. British Cycling Federation
For information on cycle racing and racing organisations:
The National Cycle Centre
1 Stuart Street, Manchester, M11 4DQ, Tel: 0161 230 2301

8. CTC (Cyclists Touring Club)
Provides advice, legal aid and insurance, and campaigns to improve facilities and opportunities for cyclists.
Publishes a very useful guide to the cycle routes of England, Wales, Scotland and Ireland that is regularly updated.
The CTC is Britain's biggest cycling organisation, with 66,000 members and affiliates. For information on touring,
technical, insurance and legal matters contact:
CTC, 69 Meadrow, Godalming, Surrey GU7 3HS Tel: 01483 417217

9. Cycle Aid
For legal advice on cycle accidents. Freephone: 0800 387815. Website: www.cycleaid.co.uk

10. Bike 1
Organises once a month, one-day circular signposted rides, mainly in the counties around Greater London.
Freepost (GI 2064), Fleet, Hampshire GU13 8B Tel: 0252 624022

11. Bike Events
Organises 10 major charity event one-day bike rides from June to October each year, including the London-Brighton
and London-Cambridge rides. Tel: 0225 310859

12. Open Air
Organises one-day charity event rides throughout the year, mainly around London, including 'To the Lighthouse' and
the London-Windsor events. Tel: 0272 227768